T0151296

The Essence of
OKINAWAN KARATE-DO

The Essence of
OKINAWAN

沖縄の空手

KARATE-DO

(Shorin-ryu)

by Shoshin Nagamine

TUTTLE Publishing
Tokyo | Rutland, Vermont | Singapore

Disclaimer: Please note that the publisher and author(s) of this instructional book are NOT RESPONSIBLE in any manner whatsoever for any injury that may result from practicing the techniques and/or following the instructions given within. Martial Arts training can be dangerous—both to you and to others—if not practiced safely. If you're in doubt as to how to proceed or whether your practice is safe, consult with a trained martial arts teacher before beginning. Since the physical activities described herein may be too strenuous in nature for some readers, it is also essential that a physician be consulted prior to training.

First paperback edition published in 1998 by Tuttle Publishing, an imprint of Periplus Editions (HK) Ltd.

www.tuttlepublishing.com

Copyright © 1976 Charles E. Tuttle Publishing, Inc.

Library of Congress Catalog Card Number: 75028717

ISBN 978-0-8048-2110-0

25 24 23 22   19 18 17 16   2206VP
Printed in Malaysia

TUTTLE PUBLISHING® is a registered trademark of Tuttle Publishing, a division of Periplus Editions (HK) Ltd.

Distributed by

North America, Latin America & Europe
Tuttle Publishing
364 Innovation Drive
North Clarendon, VT 05759-9436 U.S.A.
Tel: 1 (802) 773-8930; Fax: 1 (802) 773-6993
info@tuttlepublishing.com
www.tuttlepublishing.com

Japan
Tuttle Publishing
Yaekari Building, 3rd Floor 5-4-12 Osaki
Shinagawa-ku Tokyo 141 0032
Tel: (81) 3 5437-0171; Fax: (81) 3 5437-0755
sales@tuttle.co.jp
www.tuttle.co.jp

Asia Pacific
Berkeley Books Pte. Ltd.
3 Kallang Sector #04-01 Singapore 349278
Tel: (65) 6741-2178; Fax: (65) 6741-2179
inquiries@periplus.com.sg
www.tuttlepublishing.com

Table of Contents

Calligraphy by Koyu Shimabuku

Foreword

by JUNJI NISHIME
Member, House of Representatives
Japanese National Diet

There is a saying, one of my favorites, which reads, "Be well versed in the arts of pen and sword."

The great swordsman Musashi Miyamoto devoted his life to seeking perfection in the art of swordsmanship; at the same time, however, he developed a brilliant talent for painting. His way of life has always held a strong attraction for me.

Before the war the practice of kendo and karate was a regular part of the curriculum in secondary schools in Okinawa, contributing greatly to the training of body and spirit. It is from this viewpoint that we should consider the practice of karate, which was developed and nurtured for over a thousand years by Okinawan culture.

Shoshin Nagamine has been studying karate since the age of seventeen, and even during World War II and the period of extreme hardship which followed, he never forgot his devotion to the art of karate. His strong sense of responsibility toward karate has deeply impressed me and many others. He is truly one of the most respected masters of karate today.

Needless to say, those who are learning the art of karate will find this book invaluable. Since it is the first by an eminent Okinawan karate master on the traditions and spirit of karate-do, I wish particularly to urge young readers to study it earnestly.

Foreword

by Jugo Toma
President, Okinawa Physical Culture Ass. (1924–69)
Chief Executive, Govt. of the Ryuku Is. (1956–59)

I have long looked forward to the publication of this book. It has been one of my dreams to see it published during my lifetime. My dream has come true at last.

Karate has long been internationally recognized as a sport and martial art. I am confident that this book will contribute greatly to popularizing Okinawan karate-do and to establishing it as the purest version in forms, functions, and, most importantly, spirit.

When I was writing my memoirs, Mr. Nagamine generously offered his help by allowing me to use his research data on karate-do. During the course of our conversations, he often made profound comments on karate-do. One of them was especially impressive and imprinted itself deeply on my mind. Mr. Nagamine stated that "karate must be a defensive art from beginning to end." A great truth lies in this paradoxical maxim, which might be said to be the essence of Mr. Nagamine's philosophy of karate-do. I hope and believe that this philosophy will become a vital force in the minds of young karate devotees all over the world.

This book represents a scientific treatment of karate-do, based on genuine Okinawan tradition and on Shoshin Nagamine's deep insight and inexhaustible research. It has successfully revealed karate's true worth. It is with much pleasure, therefore, that I commend to you Shoshin Nagamine and his great work.

Preface

Karate ni sente nashi (There is no first attack in karate). This phrase, inscribed on a monument to Gichin Funakoshi in the Zen monastery of Enkakuji in Kamakura City, embodies the essence of Okinawan karate.* Karate is a martial art, yet it was developed by the Okinawans as a weaponless method of self-defense. The peculiar culture of the Okinawans, a peace-loving people desirous of living without weapons, made them raise the instinct of self-preservation to its highest form—the art of karate-do.

One of the greatest soldiers in history, Napoleon Bonaparte, upon hearing that the Okinawans carried no weapons, could only reply in astonishment, "No weapons, you mean they have no cannons?" Two Englishmen, who had traveled with the fleet to China and then to Naha, the main city of Okinawa, told Napoleon about the Okinawans on a visit to St. Helena in 1816. Napoleon could not believe that the Okinawans truly did not bear arms, and asked if they used spears or bows, or possibly knives and swords. When informed that the Okinawans carried no weapons of any kind, Napoleon exclaimed, "You mean they really carry no weapons? I cannot understand a people not interested in war."†

* Gichin Funakoshi, a famous Okinawa karate master, traveled to Japan in 1922 and taught karate there. He carried this maxim with him from Okinawa, and when he died in 1957, his students inscribed it on a monument they erected to his honor.

† Basil Hall. *Voyage to the Great Loo-Choo* (London, John Murry, 1818).

Fighting is still going on in some parts of the world today. Hardly anyone expects that the world situation can deteriorate much further without grave consequences for all. The situation, however, is extremely complicated and will not permit peace-loving countries to stop producing arms. A state of relative peace in the world seems to depend upon a delicate balance of military power among the large nations.

True world peace, however, can only be achieved when all weapons of destruction are put aside. The peaceful and weaponless Okinawans are living proof of the possibility of a world without war. All people could live in peace if they would follow the example of the Okinawans.

Men must eliminate narrow-mindedness which causes them to stand against their fellows, and acquire broad-mindedness. This is possible through the study of karate. Karate as it should be practiced is not a competitive or violent sport, where men are pitted against each other. Nor is it physical training merely for the sake of training, where the goal is merely that of smashing boards or bricks. Karate is a training of both mind and body, and leads one to a better understanding of both the self and the world.

Karate is self-training in perfection, a means whereby a man may obtain that expertise in which there is not the thickness of a hair between a man and his deed. It is a training in efficiency. It is a training in self-reliance. Its rewards are here and now, for it enables a person to meet any situation with exactly the right expenditure of effort, neither too much nor too little, and it gives him control of his otherwise wayward mind so that neither physical danger from without nor rampant passion from within can dislodge him.

In the following pages, in accordance with my understanding of the art, I have attempted to make clear what karate is and how it should be practiced. To date, no Okinawan master has set down in writing his thoughts on the theory and practice of karate-do. The art of karate has been passed from generation to generation through oral tradition and hand-to-hand teaching. I have committed my thoughts on karate to paper in the hope that the purity and essence of Okinawan karate will be preserved by its students throughout the world. I believe that the fundamental philosophy of Okinawan karate has much to impart to the world. There is hope for all mankind in the phrase *karate ni sente nashi.*

I would like to offer my deep appreciation to the following people for their efforts in the realization of this book: K. Shinzato and M. Shiroma, who translated my Japanese manuscript; F. Baehr, who assisted in the revision of the initial translation; J. Nishime, J. Toma, and Dr. Gordon Warner for their kindness in providing the forewords and recommendation; C. Omine, who acted as a technical consultant and advisor; S. Borger, who helped revise and retype the original translation; Dr. Sylvia Welch, Owen Masters and Z. Heshiki, who edited, revised, and retyped the translation into book form; D. Sampson and Mrs. Sampson, who assisted K. Shinzato in editing and revising the final transcript; and to many others who contributed their time and effort to help make this book possible.

—THE AUTHOR

The author's training hall.

PART ONE

Calligraphy (*overleaf*):
"By matching a deity in skill, you can become superhuman."

I

A Brief History of
Karate-do

Movements in karate are divided into the basics, which make up the *kata* (forms), and the intermediate techniques, which are woven into the kata for use in *kumite* (sparring). It was in Okinawa that the well-formed karate originated.

Okinawa, the main island of the Ryukyu Islands chain which stretches from Japan to Taiwan, is located some 300 miles south of the southernmost tip of the Japanese mainland, 300 nautical miles north of Taiwan, and 400 nautical miles east of China. Here the warm currents of the Yellow Sea, the East China Sea, and the Pacific Ocean meet. The island of Okinawa is small, with a total area of about 460 square miles.

Although there is evidence of recorded Okinawan history dating back 1,000 years, unfortunately no records exist that serve to give a definitive history of karate. Insufficient documentation of karate and its traditions forces its students to base their interpretation on fragmentary information gathered from historical documents and oral tradition. The brief history of karate-do which follows is my interpretation based on more than forty years of study.

THE ART OF TE

The martial arts arose out of the fundamental human instinct of self-preservation. This instinct caused primitive man, living without effective weapons in caves and trees, to defend himself from attack by using his hands, feet, or other parts of his body. The manner in which the art of self-defense developed took many forms. Boxing and wrestling

19

were created in the West. *Kempo* came out of the East, while *judo, yawara, kendo* and *aikido* originated in mainland Japan. The Okinawans developed their own unique art of self-defense; *te* literally means hands.

Most of the characteristics of Okinawan karate-do appear in the use of fists, toes, elbows, and "knife-hands." In actual practice, however, any part of the body can become a vital weapon. The use of fists, or *seiken* as employed in Okinawan karate-do, can be considered unique to it.

Kempo, yawara and other ancient forms of weaponless self-defense relied heavily on the use of "open-hand" techniques, but an historical Chinese book *Bubishi* (Martial Art Spirit), written about the use of hands in *kempo,* does refer to the merit of fists. Kanryo Higaonna (b. 1853) studied To-te (see below) for over ten years and taught To-te forms in Okinawa, but he changed the open-hand techniques to conform to the Okinawan method of using fists.

The art of *te* antedated that of karate. The literature of the Ryukyus referred to the existence of *te* before the recorded performances of practitioners of Chinese-style karate, or To-te, influenced the development of Okinawan karate in the 18th century. *Te* flourished during the golden age of Ryukyuan culture under the rule of King Shohashi in the 15th century. During this period, the Ryukyus enjoyed a rich cultural exchange with the countries of Asia, and *te* developed as it absorbed aspects of the martial arts from other countries, particularly China. That there was a difference between *te* and Chinese-style self-defense can be illustrated in both poetry and history.

A poem by the eminent Okinawan scholar Teijunsoku (also called Nago Oyakata), whose birth in 1663 antedates by ninety-eight years the first recorded performance of Chinese-style self-defense on Okinawa, mentions *te* in a very significant context. The poem reads in part:

> No matter how you may excel in the art of te,
> and in your scholastic endeavors,
> nothing is more important than your behavior
> and your humanity as observed in daily life.

History also records that a noted Okinawan karateman named Sakugawa, who lived in Shuri over two hundred years ago, learned the martial art of To-te in China. He was commonly known as To-te Sakugawa, meaning that he was a master of Chinese-style self-defense. This peculiar prefixing of the nickname "To-te" proved that among Ryukyuans there existed a unique martial art that was distinguished from To-te, or Chinese-style self-defense. Otherwise, Sakugawa would have been called *te* Sakugawa instead of To-te Sakugawa.

The development of the art of *te* accelerated with the subjugation of the Ryukyus in 1609 by the Satsuma clan of Japan. The Satsuma clan banned the use of all weapons and the practice of the martial arts by the Ryukyuans. Despite the enforcement of this ban for over three hundred years, the art of *te* was not lost. The forbidden art was passed down from father to son among the samurai class in Okinawa. Training went on in secret; devotees practiced in hidden and remote places, meeting between midnight and dawn for fear of informers. Having to study secretly and at great risk did not discourage those of martial and enterprising spirit; rather, it inspired them to greater efforts.

Not until the late 17th and early 18th century did the art of karate take shape as *te* merged with the Chinese style of self-defense to form the present-day kata of karate. Through oral tradition and hand-to-hand training, the secret performances of Chinese masters in the art of self-defense came to be known and their kata integrated with *te*. One of the most famous of these demonstrations was given by Kusanku, a Chinese expert in self-defense, in 1761. Kusanku performed with skillful use of his feet and hands, and out of this performance came the Kusanku kata, used in Matsubaya-shi-ryu, a style of the Shuri-te method of karate.

SHURI-TE AND NAHA-TE

Because of the secrecy in which *te* had to be practiced, there exists no evidence to indicate any clear-cut classifications of the various styles and types of karate during its formative years in the 18th century. Gradually, however, karate was divided into two main groups or types—Shorin-ryu or Shuri-te, and Shorei-ryu or Naha-te. Shorin-ryu developed around Shuri and Tomari, while Shorei-ryu came out of the vicinity of Naha.

The late Gichin Funakoshi, in his book *Karate-do Kyohan*, thought the characteristics of the two Okinawan karate styles indicated that they developed out of different physical requirements.* Funakoshi said that Shuri-te or Shorin-ryu was quick and fast in its movements, thus making it preferable for men of small stature whose aim was mastery of quick action. Naha-te or Shorei-ryu, on the other hand, he recommended for heavier, larger persons.

However, in the author's opinion, differences in stature and personality are not regarded as important in karate. Rather, the essence of karate lies in the process by which individuals make the utmost effort in an attempt to create limitless power by the utilization of true wisdom. The martial arts originated from the instinct of self-preservation, and ultimately aim at building a well-balanced person of sound mind and body through continuous practice. It is here that the spirit of karate-do lies.

The differences between Shuri-te and Naha-te lie in the basic movements and method of breathing. The basic approach in Shuri-te stems from certain training forms linked to natural movements. For instance, the movement of the feet, as illustrated in Fig. 1, is in a straight line when a step is taken forward or backward. Speed and proper timing is essential in the training for kicking, punching, and striking. Breathing is controlled naturally during training. No artificial breath training is necessary for a mastery of Shuri-te.

Naha-te is characterized by the steady and rooted movements as shown. Unlike the movements in Shuri-te, the feet travel rather slowly on a crescent-shaped line. In Naha-te kata there is a rhythmical, but artificial way of breathing in accordance with each of the movements. Compared to the movements in Shuri-te, Naha-te seemingly lacks swiftness in kata practice. The two schools, however, share the common factor of observing only natural stances.

Naha-te is divided into two styles—Goju-ryu and Uechi-ryu. Shuri-te is divided into three styles—two are called Shorin-ryu and a third is called Matsubayashi-ryu. I practice the Matsubayashi style of Shorin-ryu. Matsubayashi-ryu is also called Shorin-ryu. Many students are often confused because the terms are used interchangeably. The fact is that both are correct, since there can be a reading of the *kanji* (characters) taken from the Japanese language, as

* Gichin Funakoshi. *Karate-do Kyohan* (Tokyo, Kobundo Book Company, 1935). Funakoshi was founder of the Japan Karate Association.

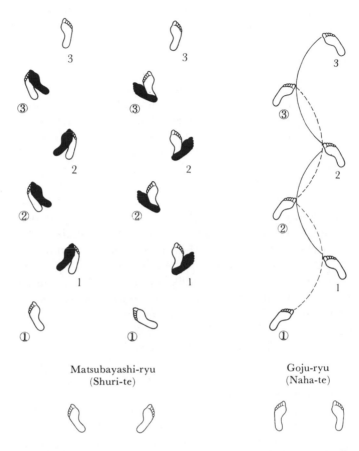

Matsubayashi-ryu
(Shuri-te)

Goju-ryu
(Naha-te)

1. Differences in the foot movements of Shuri-te and Naha-te.

松　林
matsu　*hayashi*
(pine)　(forest)
SHO　RIN

well as a reading from Chinese. Thus, the character meaning pine tree can be read as *matsu* or as *sho,* and the reading of forest can be either *hayashi* (there is a phonetic change of "h" to "b") or *rin.* Normally, my style is referred to as Shorin-ryu. When a definite distinction is desired between my style and the other styles of the Shorin family, then it is called Matsubayashi-ryu.

An old Okinawan folk song relates, "Even though we take different roads to ascend the wooden mountain, each of us can achieve our goal and appreciate the moon when we reach the top." So may we achieve the same purpose in studying karate-do whichever way we choose. The goal does not vary between the styles. In the depth of their philosophy, they share a common meaning.

POPULARIZATION OF KARATE

During the 19th century, Shuri-te and Naha-te developed further and became the unique forms of Okinawan karate. The study of karate was still confined to the samurai class and carried on in the strictest secrecy. With the end of the Satsuma occupation in 1875 and official recognition of Okinawa as part of Japan, the need for secrecy ended. Karate did not become popularly known, however, until its introduction as a physical education requirement in the Okinawan public schools in 1904. The late Anko Itosu, one of the greatest contemporary karatemen, brought about the introduction of karate into the schools, and thus made one of the most significant contributions to developing the feudalistic karate into a sport-like martial art. Itosu trained a number of eminent karatemen, among whom were Kentsu Yabu, Chomo Hanashiro, Gichin Funakoshi, Chotoku Kyan, Moden Yabiku, Choshin Chibana, Shinpan Gusukuma, Anbun Tokuda, and Kenwa Mabuni.

In 1922, Gichin Funakoshi and Choki Motobu went to Tokyo and Osaka, Japan, to ask the public's judgment on the worth of Okinawan karate. The introduction of karate into mainland Japan marked the beginning of the spread of this martial art throughout the world. In 1931 karate was officially adopted by the Nippon Butoku Kai, an organization formed to identify and systematize the martial arts of Japan. Karate thereby ceased to be just a hidden martial art utilized only within the narrow confines of Okinawa, and gained its due position among the other Japanese martial arts.

At the time of its introduction to Japan, the Okinawan martial art of self-defense was called either To-te (Chinese hands) or karate (empty hands). In the 1930s karatemen insisted that there must be a consensus on what to name this art of self-defense. At a meeting in 1936—sponsored by Chofu Ota, chief editor of the *Ryukyu Shinpo Press*—Chojun Miyagi, Chomo Hanashiro, Choki Motobu, and Chotoku Kyan agreed that the art should be called karate, meaning "an empty-handed self-defense art," or "weaponless art of self-defense."

Karate survived the holocaust of World War II and emerged to become international in scope. From the ashes of war, karate regenerated and strengthened itself to take an equal position among the international sports such as boxing, wrestling, judo, and aikido. This was truly a remarkable achievement.

When World War II ended, the U.S. Administration in Japan issued an order prohibiting the practice of judo and kendo, which were thought to foster militarism. As a result karate-do and aikido were eagerly sought after as a "safety valve" for young people's energies and the two began to draw worldwide attention. Another and more important reason for the increasing interest in karate-do and aikido was that both can be practiced without any implements. This gave an advantage under the social conditions of that time, when equipment, not only for martial arts but for any other sports, could not be acquired. Thus time and the tide were favorable for karate-do's arrival into a new era and the popularity of karate greatly increased. There arose, however, the problem of an acute shortage of qualified instructors to meet the increased demands.

Of the many karate instructors in Japan during the 1930s, only a few—notably Koyu Konishi and Shinjun Otsuka— still devoted themselves to karate-do after the war. The reasons for the instructor shortage can be attributed to the comparatively brief history of karate in Japan, war damage, and the discontinuance of karate training during the war.

Such circumstances helped to create an unusual phenomenon in Japan—the appearance of the "instant karate instructor." There are many examples and episodes concerning this phenomenon. One occurred right after the war. An Okinawan caught a thief and took him to the police. The story appeared in the newspaper, which made a big thing out of it by reporting "an Okinawan karateman" instead of "an Okinawan." The irony began after many people read the story. Young people began visiting the Okinawan to learn karate from him, a person totally unfamiliar with karate. The man became an "instant instructor." He learned karate from a real instructor by day and in the evenings taught his students what he had just learned. The man is still a master of a popular karate *dojo*, "sacred hall of learning," in Japan.

Behind the surprising development of karate-do were these instant instructors whose qualifications were unquestionably poor and insufficient. It was impossible to study karate-do under them in its traditional way, normally requiring painstaking years of learning kata. They therefore resorted to the colorful and showy free-fighting methods and techniques which anyone can practice without formal or lengthy and diligent training.

The karate clubs of some Japanese colleges were similar cases. It was difficult for the instructors of many of these college clubs to teach formal karate and to control the members, since many had already studied at various and diversified karate schools. It was found that if, under certain rules, free-fighting was emphasized in club activities, the management of the club would become easier and more effective. Considering its cause just, much of karate in Japan opted for success and popularity over content and depth. As a consequence, karate is beginning to lose its value as a martial art with the increase in worldwide popularity.

THE KUMITE MATCH

The increase in popularity can be partially attributed to the development of the karate tournament, formally called a "kumite match." On December 1, 1963, an All-Japan Karate-do Championship Tournament was held in Tokyo. It was a big event, with more than a hundred teams and many individuals competing. The rules for that tournament are still appropriate today. Article 3 of the rules authorized three fundamental *waza* (techniques) to be used: *tsuki waza* (punching), *uchi waza* (striking), and *keri waza* (kicking). In order to simplify the judgment of the referees, *kaikoken* (four finger extended mid-knuckle fist) and *nakatakaken* (midfinger extended knuckle fist) were included in *tsuki waza;* *shuto* (knife-hand), *kasane uchi* (double knife-hand), *haito* (reverse knife-hand), and *furitsuki* (roundhouse punch) were included in *uchi waza;* and *kansetsu-geri* (kicks aiming at joints) and *yoko-geri* (foot edge) were included in *keri waza.* The first provision of Article 4 of the rules further stated that a point would be given when an attack was made to a crucial point of the body with correct form and with the proper *ma-ai* and *kiai. Ma-ai* refers to the proper and advantageous distance for defensive and offensive purposes between opponents in prearranged *kumite* or actual fighting situations. A further discussion of *ma-ai* will be found in Chapter VI (p. 246) *Kiai* literally means "spirit convergence" or "energy concentration," taking advantage of a sound to fuse the maximum efficient force that can be exerted. When using *kiai*, one is using the utmost life force.

Carefully studying the rules, one can quite easily see why *uraken* (backfist strike) and *hiji-ate* (elbow smash) were excluded, even though they are, in actual fighting, rich in their variety of attacks and important in the sense that they can be utilized frequently, regardless of the distance between opponents. The only possible reason for the exclusion of these effective *waza* from *kime waza* (winning techniques) in the tournament system would be for simplifying the referees' judgments. These dangerously effective *waza* were excluded only because the Japanese karate authorities wished to develop the tournament system with the least hindrance.

According to the provisions, the judgment of victory or defeat is based totally on the subjective decision of the two referees. Often, however, contestants do not consider themselves beaten, even though the decision goes against them, and they feel frustrated at the judgment. This dissatisfaction seldom occurs in other sports such as judo, boxing and wrestling. Almost every karate tournament is punctuated with complaints. A member of a college karate club once told me that in a tournament with five members, when the first three had been defeated, the remaining two did something violent to beat the opposing team, deliberately ignoring the rules.

Effects of the Tournament System

As a result of the tournament system, many are urged to employ not just hard, but savage training in order to defeat opponents. At some college clubs in Japan, the attitude of juniors toward seniors is the same as was that of soldiers toward their officers in the old Japanese army, where brutality predominated. It could even be worse, for in the army officers were forced to follow a stricter discipline than the soldiers themselves. At the college clubs, it is acknowledged that a freshman is treated as a slave; a sophomore, a peasant; a junior, an ordinary man; and a senior, a god.

Seniors are apt to train their juniors brutally without participating in the training themselves. They seem to regard cruelty as strictness, and are under the illusion that they are engaged in hard training, although they are only satiating their savageness.

On July 18, 1970, a member of a college karate club in Tokyo was killed by other members as the result of *shigoki* (savage training). This tragic mishap emphasizes a mistaken concept about the need and importance of "guts" in karate training. In the hierarchy of the college karate club, humanism is being neglected. When a member wanted to escape from this mad world and proposed to quit the club, he was forced to undergo a last *shigoki* and was killed. The most significant aspect of this incident is that it was not just accidental. What is happening in some of those clubs in Japan is a complete negation of the pursuit of the genuine spirit of karate-do. This, it seems, is the natural outgrowth of the adoption of the tournament system into karate-do.

The tournament rules used in 1963 have been revised several times. The revisions, however, were only minor and the major defect, in which victory or defeat is totally based on the decision of the referees, remains unchanged.

That ancient Japanese arts such as kenjutsu and jujutsu were able to be transformed into modern sports like judo and kendo is based upon two important factors: victory or defeat is easily decided, and the danger of being injured can be avoided. A karate tournament, on the contrary, lacks these important sports essentials. Many contestants have been injured in karate tournaments because it is extremely difficult for contestants to stop their *tsuki* or *keri* before it reaches the opponent's body, though the rules require that it should be stopped. The two contestants are not still, but in constantly violent movement, eager to attack each other and to evade the opponent's attack. Therefore, it is not surprising that they often receive direct blows or kicks to their bodies, even though they try to prevent injury. The fact is, danger is increasing at tournaments.

It would be illogical to conclude that since tournament-centered karate finally succeeded in achieving popularity in Japan, a tournament system should be adopted to popularize Okinawan karate-do.

The value of the tournament system has in fact been recently questioned by some local journalists and even some karate masters. They have voiced the opinion that the wide and rapid popularization of karate has come about because karatemen in Japan boldly forsook the traditional kata-centered karate-do and turned karate into a sport by employing the tournament system. They feel that if Okinawan karate clings to a kata-centered karate-do, it will inevitably be forced to lose its authoritative position as the center of karate.

Unless methods are devised to make contest decisions clear and easy, and to eliminate danger, the author recommends the study and practice of karate, not as a sport, but as a martial art *(budo)*, and the development as such.

RECOMMENDATIONS FOR STUDY

The following are important recommendations and mottoes under which karate-do should be learned and practiced:

1. Develop karate-do on the basis of its history and tradition.

2. Study and practice kata strictly and correctly. (In order to focus all possible strength into each movement of the kata, constant repetition is required. The body must be thoroughly trained, and this takes many years. Even after many years, kata practice is never finished, for there is always something new to be learned about executing a movement.)

3. Study and practice kumite (formalized and free-fighting), not primarily for tournament purposes, but to acquire *ma-ai,* to develop the martial art sense of reading the opponent's movements, and to develop *kiai* and stamina, which cannot be fully attained through the practice of kata alone.

4. Fully utilize such methods as rope-skipping, exercise with bar bells, dumbbells, *chishi* (an ancient form of dumbbell), *sashi* (iron hand-grip), etc., to develop the muscles and physical power.

5. Study the use of *makiwara* from every possible angle in order to develop *atemi,* concentrated destructive power. This force is manifested in such demonstrations as the breaking of boards, tiles, or bricks with the hands or feet. (See Chapter VI, p. 249.)

6. Include *zazen* (Zen training in a sitting position) in karate practice for further mind training and understanding of the essence of karate-do and Zen as one.

The author has devoted his life to the study of karate-do based on the above ideas and principles, and will do so for the rest of his life.

In conclusion, let us remember that in some cases, it is permissible to revise ancient arts to make them modern and popular. However, it is also dangerous and unwise to reject old things just because they are old. Karate was created by our ancestors and throughout its long history from generation to generation, it has conquered many difficulties and survived with its essential spirit intact. Karate, like all things classical, has the potential to meet the demands of various ages and to produce something new out of itself without rejecting those basic elements upon which it was founded. The formal training methods of the great masters of the past must be observed because karate was meant to be pursued as a martial art, not a sport where the goal is defeating an opponent or winning points. Karate has an ancient heritage, full of wisdom. Let us follow the way of karate as shown to us by the masters.

II

My Life with Karate

A Prescription for Health

My life with karate began in my seventeenth year. Born on July 15, 1907, in Tomari, Naha City, Okinawa, I spent my childhood plagued with ill health. When I was a sophomore in high school, I contracted a gastroenteric disorder that was so serious my doctor was unable to cure me, and my friends feared that I might have tuberculosis. I decided to go on a self-imposed diet and take up the study of karate under Chojin Kuba, who lived in my neighborhood.

I found that karate gradually improved my health. At the age of nineteen, I undertook the study of karate in earnest and entered a school in Shuri under the direction of Taro Shimabuku. With the encouragement of Shimabuku and hard training on my part, karate came to fascinate me so much that I would often forget to eat. On Shimabuku's recommendation, I studied under Sensei Ankichi Arakaki. Both Shimabuku and I became Sensei Arakaki's students. Under Arakaki's guidance, I began to appreciate the spirit and beauty of karate-do.

By the time of my senior year in high school, I had become the captain of the school's karate club. Not only had I recovered from the stomach disease, but I had also grown much stronger. My friends even nicknamed me Chippaii Matsu (tenacious pine tree). That year my school participated in a karate demonstration in Naha. In order to participate, we had to train every evening with the eminent karateman Kodatsu Iha, one of the direct disciples of the

31

The author at 19 (1925)   at 22 (1928)   at 31 (1937)

great Kosaku Matsumora. I remember that Iha was very strict, but was also a very kind instructor.

After high school, my much improved health enabled me to pass the physical examination for draftees. I was assigned to a Japanese artillery unit that was sent to China in 1928. While stationed there, I hoped to learn Chinese kempo. I could not pursue my wish, however, and was only able to obtain an instruction book on the Chinese martial arts.

After I was discharged from military service, I thought about my future work. I finally determined that the police force was the only place where I could study karate further and, at the same time, make the most use of karate while on the job. In December 1931, I received a very timely appointment to become a policeman in Okinawa. I regarded the police force as the best position for me because I was enthusiastic about scientifically studying Okinawan karate, which had not been systematized, and about training mind and body through karate.

My appointment to the Kadena Police Station from 1931 to 1935 enabled me to take karate instruction from the famous Chotoku Kyan, known locally as Chan Mi-gwa (small-eyed Kyan). In 1936, while studying at the Tokyo Metropolitan Police Academy, I was taught by Choki Motobu, called Motobu-zaru (Motobu the monkey) because of his great agility. He was known as one of the greatest karatemen of Okinawa.

at 46 (1952)   at 54 (1960)   at 65 (1971)

At the Japanese Martial Arts Festival in Kyoto in May 1940, at the age of thirty-five, I successfully passed the qualifying examinations for karate instructor and received the degree of Renshi (Qualified Instructor of Karate). On this occasion, I also received the third degree of kendo, in the Japanese art of sword fighting, which I had begun to study four years earlier.

Later I became a member of the Okinawa Police Kendo Team, and in 1943, I went to Nagasaki, Japan, to participate in the Kyushu District Police Kendo Tournament. I studied kendo zealously because I wanted to get at the heart of the similarities between kendo and karate.

During World War II, I was assigned to be chief of the Emergency War Supply Distribution Department of the Naha Police Station. With the escalation of the war, we were pushed back to the southern tip of the island, across from the Shuri area. On June 27, 1945, the Japanese Commander, Lieutenant General Ushijima, faithful to the traditional samurai code, committed hara-kiri at a cave in Mabuni, or what is now called "Suicide Cliff." Ushijima left a poem before he killed himself. It read in part: "Although young leaves are going to fall before autumn, I hope they will grow once again when spring comes to the island in the future." At the news of Ushijima's death, we voluntarily surrendered to the United States Army, believing that there was no meaning in fighting any longer.

After the surrender, I was sent to a village called Iraha, where I did odd jobs for the wounded at a hospital in the rear. One day, I happened to find a book in the street. To my surprise, it was the *Karate-do Kyohan* by Gichin Funakoshi, who first introduced karate into Japan. I felt it was more than a coincidence that I should come across this book, believing then that I was directed to take the "way of karate" by fate. I decided to devote myself to karate-do to help reform the decadent society that had arisen in the wake of war.

After the war, the young people were driven to despair; their sense of morality vanished and juvenile delinquency soared. To instil an undying faith in the hearts and minds of promising youth seemed imperative, and I felt there was a real need for a karate *dojo* in which young people could train their bodies and build indomitable spirits.

The state of our ruined country prevented me from realizing immediately my dream of a *dojo,* and I returned to the police department. In January 1951, I was promoted to Police Superintendent and appointed head of the Motobu Police Station.

After assuming my duties there, I planned a whole year's schedule for instructing judo systematically for all young white belt policemen for the purpose of participating in an All-Okinawan Judo Tournament. I began to train them each day, also letting them practice karate.

During that year, I faced many difficulties, the worst of which was the death of one of my fellow policemen as a result of a judo accident. After overcoming many difficulties, we finally participated in the judo tournament in October, and our white belt team from the Motobu Police Station, which had only sixty policemen, won against thirteen other larger police teams. Some of these teams, for example, from Maehara, Koza, Shuri, and Naha stations, had more than two hundred policemen each. But our hard training of the previous year resulted in our victory at this tournament. As a symbol of our victory, all our white belt men were awarded black belts of the first degree.

Pleased with the result of my efforts as the head of the Motobu Police Station, I resigned from the post to pursue my main purpose of building a karate *dojo*. Realizing my dreams, I built my *dojo* in Naha in January 1953, and named it Kodokan Karate-do and Kobujutsu Dojo ("kobu-jutsu" means old Okinawan martial arts that use ancient-style weapons).

The story of my life with karate must include the role of my teachers and their influence, not only upon myself, but upon all who follow their way. I received instruction from three great teachers: Ankichi Arakaki, Chotoku Kyan, and Choki Motobu. Sensei Kyan had been a student of Sensei Sokon Matsumura of Shuri, and Sensei Motobu had studied under Sensei Kosaku Matsumura of Tomari. Therefore, I am the third instructor, following these two men. Since my teachings are based on the ideas of these two noted masters, I decided in 1947 to adopt the name Matsubayashi-ryu in honor of both of them. In this way, the names of these karatemen are retained in our minds.

Insights of Arakaki

My first master, when I was still a teen-ager, was Sensei Ankichi Arakaki. Arakaki showed me the integral relationship between karate and Okinawan culture, and opened my mind to the beauty of karate as an art. Although Arakaki lived to be only twenty-eight, his influence on the development of karate as an art was enormous.

Ankichi Arakaki was born in November 1899 in Shuri, the first son in a family of eleven children born to a sakè (rice wine) brewer. He was a quiet but bright boy in elementary school. In junior high school, however, he began to neglect his studies in favor of sports and eventually had to quit school.

Arakaki began to study karate early in his boyhood. His first teachers were Shinpan Gusukuma and Chomo Hana-shiro. After quitting school, he studied under Choshin Chibana, who later brought honor to the Okinawan karate world when he received Emperor Hirohito's Fourth Order of Merit.

Arakaki was not a large man, but he was sturdy and had an inborn ability for sports. Because his family was rich, he could afford to put his heart and soul into karate practice. Within a few years, he gained a reputation as a good karate-man.

At the age of nineteen, Arakaki's agility and strength came to the public's notice. In that year, Arakaki partici-

Ankichi Arakaki

pated in a sumo wrestling tournament in Shuri. He was matched against a notorious giant wrestler from Yomitan village. The audience naturally believed that Arakaki would be defeated easily, but surprisingly, he defeated his giant opponent with hidden strength and ingenuity.

Another unusual episode in Arakaki's life is told by Chojo Oyama, former mayor of Okinawa (Koza) City, who was one year Arakaki's senior in the elite Tokyo Metropolitan Honor Guard Battalion, which Arakaki joined when he was twenty. When the division was holding a river-crossing exercise, the soldiers were ordered to dive into the Tonè River, one of the swiftest and most dangerous in Japan, and to carry a rope to a small boat floating two miles up river. After securing the boat, the soldier then had to return to the bank. Arakaki was the first man to come back among the few who completed the feat. The other soldiers praised him for bravery, and regarded in a new light the spirit of karate which had enabled Arakaki to reach extraordinary heights of bravery and endurance.

Upon discharge from military service in 1921, Arakaki moved to the village of Kadena, where he had the opportunity to learn karate from Chotoku Kyan, another of the great karatemen in Okinawa. It was very fortunate for both karatemen to meet at that time, for at fifty-five, Kyan was a perfect master for the young and promising Arakaki.

When I was twenty years old, I was recommended to Arakaki (then twenty-eight) by my former sensei, Taro Shimabuku. Arakaki's scientific explanations and historical allusions made his karate teaching fascinating to me; when

I came back to him after an eighteen-month absence for military service, I was even more impressed with his broad knowledge of karate and his scientific attitude, not only toward karate, but all the martial arts.

Arakaki's keen insight into the merits of our heritage, at a time when most Okinawans underestimated the value of their culture, impressed me deeply. He was not only a student of karate but a student of the arts. For example, he pointed out to his students that both karate and Ryukyuan dancing showed similarities in their movements from the viewpoint of dynamics. Karate, however, originated, as Arakaki wanted us to understand fully, from man's instinct for self-preservation, while dancing developed from man's desire to express his emotions. A karateman, Arakaki advised, would comprehend the differences and similarities between the two by studying dancing.

Arakaki himself could dance well. He once performed the *saru-mai* (monkey dance), one of the most difficult classical dances. In it, he climbed a pole on the stage and came down head first, doing cartwheels. His movements were light, fast, and precise, and so harmonious with the music that the exquisite performance remained long in the audience's memory.

Not only· could Arakaki dance well, but he also had a profound knowledge of the classical plays of Okinawa and was well-versed in poetry. He was truly a Renaissance man. Under his influence, I began to study dance and poetry.

Because of his father's death at a time of declining family fortunes in the economic crisis following World War I, Arakaki had to confront the financial difficulties of his family and try to retrieve its losses. The hardships were tremendous, and he fell ill and died of ulcers on December 28, 1927.

Although death cut short Arakaki's promising career, his accomplishments will live as long as karate-do exists. His teaching contributed immeasurably to the establishment of karate-do as an art.

The story of Arakaki's life is not complete without describing, albeit briefly, his specialty in *waza*. We can learn much from his devotion and enthusiasm for karate.

Arakaki began to learn kata from Masters Chibana and Shiroma as a young boy. Because of his family's wealth, he had no difficulty in finding time for intense karate practice.

His innate genius for budo and superb coordination enabled him to master almost anything he encountered. His constant and strenuous efforts, combined with his enthusiasm, would have brought him world recognition as a master of karate and inventor of his unique *tsumasaki-geri* (toe-tip.kick).

Although Arakaki devoted time to other sports during his high school years, his true interest was karate. Whatever he did, it was for karate. He practiced judo, sumo, swimming. He climbed trees, and walked tip-toe—all to strengthen himself for karate. After a year of total dedication to the training of *nidan-geri* (flying front kick) and *tsumasaki-geri* (toe-tip kick), Arakaki mastered his own unique style of *tsumasaki-geri*. No other karateman could match his speed and power in this technique.

Two episodes in Arakaki's life can serve to illustrate the power of his *tsumasaki-geri*. The first occurred when he was nineteen years old. One day, while at a tea house with friends, he was provoked by a huge man well over six feet tall. Arakaki tried to ignore the man. The man then pushed Arakaki down the stairs. He rolled down in a ball, then lay at the bottom without stirring to catch his breath. The man, still taunting Arakaki, rushed down and attempted to entangle his arms and legs. At this, Arakaki finally lost patience, and gave a kick to the man's body; with a deep groan, the man sank to the floor.

About a half a year later, a newspaper article reported that a giant sumo wrestler had died of a hemorrhage of the lungs. The article also stated that the actual cause of death was suspected to be a kick in the abdomen given by a certain karateman six months earlier. Of course, the truth was not easy to ascertain, and even the police were reluctant to investigate the matter. One thing seemed likely, however; Arakaki's kick was lethal.

Another story of Arakaki's strength went like this: his brother, Ansuke, showed no enthusiasm for budo; in fact, he disliked it. One day Ansuke, desperately wanting money for sakè, recklessly challenged Arakaki, saying he could try a kick at him for so much money. Realizing Ansuke's desire for money, Arakaki accepted the challenge in a brotherly way. As can be easily guessed, Sensei must have kicked his brother as lightly as he could. That night, though, Ansuke ran a fever, and he had to have an operation on his thigh several days later.

Chotoku Kyan

Inspiration from Kyan

The second of my masters was Kyan, who was born in December 1870, the third son of the Kyans who were the 11th descendants of King Shosei of the Ryukyu Kingdom. His father, Chofu Kyan, held the post of steward to the family of Sir Shotai, the last of Ryukyu royal lineage. Chofu Kyan was well-versed in Chinese classics and Japanese arts and letters; he was also an excellent karateman. Sir Shotai so deeply trusted him, because of his serious personality and his accomplishments in the arts of pen and sword, that he gave Chofu the responsibility of carrying on all the business of the Shotai family.

At the age of twelve, Chotoku Kyan went to Tokyo with his father and studied Chinese classics until he was sixteen. Compared with his father, he was rather small and in poor health. It seemed to his father that his son's health should be improved so that he might become an honorable samurai and descendant of the Shosei royal lineage. Therefore, he often took Chotoku outdoors on cold winter days to train him in Sumo and karate wrestling.

Chotoku came back to Okinawa after his father finished his duty as a steward in Tokyo. When Chotoku was about twenty years old, his father felt it necessary for him to practice karate regularly. And it was his father who gave him some very important advice about how to turn his weakness to advantage: "You are not blessed with physical constitution, yet you have pluck more than sufficient to conquer your physical handicaps. Furthermore, success in budo does not necessarily rely on how you are built; rather, it depends on how strenuously you try to train yourself. The most important thing is to master one *waza* which is best adapted to your physical constitution. Then you can be self-confident enough to believe that you are second to none as far as budo is concerned."

At that time in the karate world of Okinawa, there were three noted karatemen: Sokon Matsumura in Shuri, Anko Itosu, also in Shuri, and Pechin Oyadomari in Naha. Chotoku's father asked the three of them to train his son in karate. He asked them, not because he could not teach his son himself, but because he knew he loved his son too much to be severe enough in karate exercises.

Kyan learned karate rapidly, absorbing both Tomari-te and Shuri-te. Within a few years, he had mastered the secrets of karate which could be used most effectively by a small man like himself. The secret was that when a small man faces an opponent, he must not take backward steps to evade blows or kicks; instead he should take forward steps or side steps so that he can take the offensive right after defending himself. To acquire this "offense-right-after-defense" technique by stepping forward or sideways, Kyan used to train himself on the banks of the Hija River, keeping his back to the river or the railings of the bridge.

In Kyan's younger days, young men were apt to be easily carried away by youthful ardor and were willing to try out the art of karate in actual fights. As a matter of fact, Kyan was very often challenged. Although he consequently had to fight very often, no one ever heard that he was beaten. By the time he was thirty years old, he had become distinguished throughout Shuri and Naha. His achievements are even more remarkable when considered in the light of his family's personal difficulties.

Because of the reform of the social system under the Meiji government, most of the lords and samurai were deprived of their social privileges and economic supports, and sank into poverty. Among those who fell on hard times were members of Kyan's family. They were forced to move to the village of Yomitan, where they owned a small amount of property. Kyan had to struggle for a living by doing such odd jobs as raising silkworms and pulling carts. In spite of his miserable life, the thought of giving up the study of karate was the furthest thing from his mind.

Under these depressing circumstances, Kyan mastered

the form Kusanku from a karate expert named Yara, well-known in the area of Yomitan.

The success of Kyan's training can be clearly seen in the following episode, which occurred when he was a wagon driver at the age of forty. There was a large, powerful young man called Matsuda, who made a habit of teasing and picking on youngsters in the village. When Kyan reproached Matsuda for his bullying, Matsuda turned his anger on Kyan and challenged him. He asserted that even if Kyan were a renowned karate master, he would be nothing in a real fight. Matsuda went too far when he told Kyan that his defeat would prove that karate was one thing and actual fighting another. Kyan accepted the challenge.

The two fought in a vacant lot by the Hija River. Kyan stood with *shizentai-dachi* (natural stance), keeping his back to the river. When Matsuda tried to deliver a blow to Kyan's abdomen as though to strike *makiwara*, Kyan instantly shifted his position to evade the attack and simultaneously kicked the outer part of Matsuda's thigh. Matsuda flew spinning into the river. He emerged a chastened man.

In addition to his mastery of Kusanku, Kyan also invented a special *jodan-zuki* (upper punch). Kyan fully realized his own handicap and turned it to advantage by means of hard training and creativity.

Later Kyan taught karate to the young people of the village and gave instruction at the Kadena Police Station and other places. At that time, I was assigned to the Kadena Police Station, and fortunately had an opportunity to study Kyan's favorite forms of Passai, Chinto, and Kusanku which I had previously learned under Shimabuku and Arakaki.

In May 1942, at the opening of my first *dojo*, the only karate school opened formally in Naha City, Kyan demonstrated his favorite form of karate, Passai, and *bo-jutsu* (art of *bo*) before such honorable guests as Rear Admiral Kenwa Kanna; Kowa Matayoshi, the former chief editor of the *Ryukyu Shinpo Press;* a dentist, Hidehiko Tomoyose; and Ansei Arakaki, a brother of Ankichi Arakaki. His beautiful performance at the age of seventy-three could still exalt his audience to the quintessence of karate-do and leave them spellbound. This amazing and memorable performance was to be his last. Kyan passed away on the northern part of Okinawa on September 20, 1945, at the age of seventy-six.

It can be said that he lived a natural span of life, considering the depressed and desperate situation in devastated Okinawa right after World War II. Perhaps this proves that Kyan never allowed opponents to injure him directly, so excellent was his art of karate.

Kyan often said to me, "A mastery of karate does not depend on the learner's physical constitution, but mainly on constant practice." One of the examples he gave concerned the development of fists: "The daily practice of *makiwara* striking can produce power destructive enough to break boards or bricks, but powerful fists can easily be weakened through negligence of constant practice." As anyone can see, this is true about karate practice as a whole. Constant hard work and a strong will are the only ways to make a student of karate achieve the secrets and beauties of karate-do. "Merely an excellent physical constitution cannot guarantee a mastery of karate-do." These remarks took root in my mind and made me what I am today, even though I was once handicapped physically for karate. I consider myself lucky and privileged to have been able to learn so many important things from Kyan's theory of karate training.

KUMITE DEVELOPMENT UNDER MOTOBU

The third of my noted teachers was Choki Motobu. Motobu was born in Shuri in February, 1871, the third son of a high ranking *aji,* or lord.

Because the tendency of the time was to neglect the education of all but the first-born son, Choki and his brothers were ignored in favor of the eldest. The elder brother, Choyu, designated to carry on his family's heritage, received the excellent education and training in the martial arts that befitted a samurai.

Without the education his brother was given, Choki Motobu grew to be a man of rough character whose chief ambition was to be the strongest in Okinawa. In an attempt to realize this ambition, he trained by himself and engaged in *makiwara* striking exercises and heavy rock lifting. He learned much on his own, and his ability to move quickly and nimbly earned him the name Motobu the monkey.

In the evenings, Motobu made it a habit to go to the entertainment district where he would start fights to test his prowess. He was once badly defeated when he challenged a karate expert called Itarashiki, who disposed of him as

Choki Motobu

though he were a child. Although galled by this defeat, he was so enthusiastic about karate practice that he intensified his efforts, continuing to pick fights and learning new fighting techniques from his opponents. Most of the karate masters at that time were highly critical of Motobu's aggressive attitude and his reckless manner of learning karate by street fighting, and they refused to teach him. One karateman, however, Kosaku Matsumora of Tomari, was impressed by Motobu's enthusiasm for karate and taught him Naihanchi and Passai.

Motobu also asked Matsumora to teach him the art of kumite. Since kumite is directly linked to actual fighting, Matsumora was afraid that Motobu might use it in the street. He refused him, telling him to study fighting techniques on his own. But Motobu didn't give up. According to the late Ryojin Kin, the distinguished master of Ryukyuan music, Motobu studied Matsumora's kumite by secretly watching him nightly through the fence around the *dojo*.

Not until Motobu was well into middle age did he achieve popular recognition as a powerful karateman. It happened soon after Motobu moved to Osaka in 1921. He himself told me the story of how all Japan came to know of Motobu-zaru.

On a trip to Kyoto, Motobu and a friend witnessed a contest in which amateur participants from any martial art were invited to pit themselves against the professional boxers. After a few matches, there appeared a foreign professional, about six feet tall, whose arrogant tone was clearly understood despite his foreign tongue. A referee announced that any challenger would be welcome against the foreigner, with a prize for the winner.

No one came forward. The foreigner became more arrogant, so much so that Motobu's friend urged him to challenge the boxer, adding that he would bet on Motobu. Motobu stepped into the ring, his fighting spirit aroused by this new challenge.

The boxer was taken aback by Motobu's strange fighting stance and small stature, but he made the mistake of regarding him as a "kid." For two rounds he circled Motobu with a disdainful smile. In the third round Motobu realized that the boxer was making fun of him and changed to the offensive. The audience heard a sharp *kiai* by Motobu and the boxer fell to the floor. Beside the big body lying in the ring, little Motobu stood nonchalantly. The fight was certainly over, but nobody knew what had happened. There were whispers among the spellbound audience. They asked each other, "What was that? Is that *yawara*? It doesn't look like . . ." As a matter of fact, with his lightning-like karate-hand, Motobu had struck his opponent's temple with such speed that the audience was unaware of it. Motobu was fifty-two when he fought the boxer.

This extraordinary occurrence caused a sensation among the public, and the story of Motobu-zaru appeared in a popular magazine, making him known throughout the country. As a result, Motobu began to teach karate in Osaka and opened a karate *dojo* in Tokyo. He was eventually asked to teach at universities.

If Motobu's aggression seems difficult to understand after I have said that the essence of karate is that there is no first attack, the Western reader must remember that the Orient has only recently come out of the feudal age. The need to test one's self, to pit one's self against an opponent was part of the feudal ethic. Feudalism did not begin to wane in the Orient until contact with the industrialized West was established in the 19th century. (Even now, the feudal ethic, with its aggressive attitudes, is not completely dead.) Motobu was born in an age when the need to prove one's self in combat was still part of the mentality of the Orient.

Later in his life, Motobu put aside aggression and studied karate to seek its true spirit—conquest of self, and not others. The change in Motobu's attitude is illuminating and inspiring. We can learn much in his switch from an aggressively violent man who had become famous through his mastery of fighting skills to a seeker who concentrated on the kata to find the true essence of karate-do.

I had an opportunity to receive instruction for six months from Motobu while I was studying at the Tokyo Metropolitan Police Station as an exchange student from Okinawa in 1936. Motobu was happy to see the spread of karate-do in Tokyo, but at the same time, he deplored the fact that many of Okinawa's traditional karate forms were being changed from the original to modernized ones. He also told me he would like to return to Okinawa to master the Okinawan karate forms while his senior, Kentsu Yabu, was still alive, so that he might pass on the correct, original Okinawan forms. True to his words, Motobu went back to Okinawa later in 1936 and visited all his masters to discuss the situation of karate-do in Tokyo. He examined the original Okinawan karate forms and the kobujutsu forms (kata with ancient style weapons) and then returned to Tokyo.

Motobu did not develop his mastery of karate only by fighting. He combined what he had learned in fighting with a mastery of kata, which came only after long practice and work with instructors like Matsumora. Because Motobu's style developed as a balance between kata and kumite, it was unique. For instance, the position of his hands in the postures of *tsukiwaza* and *keriwaza* was a bit higher than that of other karate schools—Shuri-te and Tomari-te. He also posed the knuckle just below the breast and beside the lung.

One of Motobu's specialties was *keikoken-zuki* (forefinger-knuckle punch). Motobu always attached great importance to the use of *makiwara* in karate training. There are no karatemen who do not use *makiwara*, but the difference between Motobu and the others was that he could strike *makiwara* with *keikoken*. No other karateman in the history of Okinawan karate has ever matched Motobu in the destructive power of *keikoken*. Motobu's theory for evaluating *keikoken*'s importance was drawn from his rich experiences in actual fighting. "In actual fighting, you must get close to the opponent in order to give him a fatal blow. However, when you get too close to the opponent, you can't use *seiken* properly and effectively. In this case, either *keikoken* or *uraken* can produce the most vitally destructive power." Thus asserted Motobu, and the assertion was beautifully justified by his own karate.

Just before World War II, Motobu returned to Okinawa. On September 2, 1944, he died of a stomach disease in Naha at the age of seventy-three. After I had personal instruction from Motobu and learned kumite from him late in his life, my old ideas on kumite were changed. I was inspired to create new ideas, based on the instruction of this teacher, who learned kumite through his own experience in actual fights. I have always been encouraged by his way of life sustained by his strong will and his devotion to karate-do.

I owe a great deal of what I have achieved in the course of my career as a karateman to Motobu's karate-do and his teaching. Without him, I could never have developed seven kata of kumite, which are the basic forms of kumite in Matsubayashi-ryu.

The reader may now understand, through the relation of my life with karate and that of my masters, that my teachers and I never innovated for any purpose except to preserve and advance karate as a martial art, practical for personal defense, and highly valuable as a way to self-understanding.

III

Thoughts on the Mastery of Karate-do

The mastery of karate-do requires dedication and strenuous effort. To pursue karate means to seek to master one's self. The true study of karate must transcend the mere physical —it must become a way of life.

Before I describe the physical aspects—the movements in the various sequences in Matsubayashi-ryu—I would like the student to be aware of the spiritual aspects of karate training. The following precepts and maxims should serve as a guide to what karate truly is.

PRECEPTS IN THE MASTERY

1. He is human and so am I.

2. I cannot develop my own potentialities when in the trap of self-limitation.

3. I must discard this self-limitation. If he practices three times, I must practice six times.

4. "Do not be dependent upon others for your improvement." Musashi Miyamoto, Japan's greatest swordsman, once said, "Pay your respects to the Gods and Buddhas, but never rely on them."

5. Earnestly cultivate your mind as well as your body and believe in yourself.

6. Karate-do may be referred to as the conflict within yourself, or a life-long marathon which can be won only through self-discipline, hard training, and your own creative efforts.

1. *Courtesy:* Karate begins with courtesy and ends with it. No one is qualified to be a karateman without courtesy even if he excels others in his technique. Courtesy means always asking yourself whether you are pursuing karate-do for the purpose of seeking peace and showing your deep respect for others. That is why the practice or demonstration of kata begins and ends with a bow. The bow represents one's recognition of the true meaning of courtesy.

When we pursue karate-do, we try to learn the theory and its application from our predecessors and senior karatemen with respect and courtesy. On their part, they teach us with due regard and consideration, yet with strictness. We must respect this sort of mutualism in which an open-minded relationship between senior and junior karatemen is observed. This, too, is what we call courtesy.

2. *Cleanliness:* A karateman must always try to keep his body and mind clean and right. Once he loses his righteous and pure mind, it is no longer possible for him to learn karate for the right purpose. Once he lacks cleanliness, it is no longer possible for him to concentrate on karate practice. In this connection he should learn something important from the following proverb: "There is no reformation of yourself without keeping yourself clean, and no cleanliness without keeping your mind right."

3. *Diligence:* Steady and hard efforts can produce miracles, as we can see in the example of Japan's miraculous economic restoration from the ashes of war. Traditionally, the Japanese are a hard-working race. This national trait enabled them to achieve the prosperity that Japan now enjoys.

As diligence is firmly rooted in the spirit of bushido (way of martial arts), so we must bestow it on our younger generation so they may overcome the difficult situations they encounter.

ATTITUDES TO BE KEPT FOR KARATE TRAINING

1. Karate begins with courtesy and ends with it. Therefore, we must be courteous to seniors, juniors, friends, and even foes. We must first purify our minds and always be mentally and physically sound.

2. We must sweep from our minds all egocentric and preoccupying thoughts during practice, concentrating on all the movements with maximum vigor. When this is done, karate ultimately produces in the individual a vital concentration of energy that expands to heroic proportions in times of crisis.

3. Karate requires a harmony between breath and action. Therefore, we must learn to adjust our breathing until we reach the point where each breath coincides with each of the movements during practice.

4. Karate requires a perfect finish at the end of each kata performance. Therefore, we must complete each kata practice with full mind and maximum power.

5. Karate practice must be finished by observing the essential idea that karate begins and ends with courtesy. Therefore, we must end practice by bowing with decorum.

THE ETHICS OF THE DOJO

1. First, purify your mind.

2. Cultivate the power of perseverance by strengthening your body and overcoming the difficulties that arise during training.

3. The *dojo* is the place where courage is fostered and superior human nature is bred through the ecstasy of sweating in hard work. It is the sacred place where the human spirit is polished.

4. Seniors and black belts are well aware of these facts. Therefore, beginners are requested to help make the *dojo* a sacred place by keeping in mind the above precepts and observing the following:

Always keep *karate-gi* (uniforms) clean.
Help clean the changing room, shower, reception room, and portal.
Be well-versed in the "Precepts for Mastering Karate-do."
Be sure to place the training equipment where it belongs after use.

TRAINING HINTS

1. *Vital Parts of the Body:* The vital parts of our body are the vulnerable nerve-centered parts.

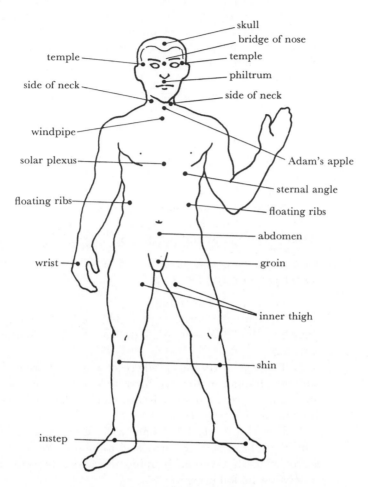

temple

side of neck

windpipe

solar plexus

floating ribs

wrist

instep

skull

bridge of nose

temple

philtrum

side of neck

Adam's apple

sternal angle

floating ribs

abdomen

groin

inner thigh

shin

Vital parts of the body.

These parts can suffer a mortal wound by a powerful blow. Therefore, it is necessary for a karate student to have some knowledge of them.

2. *Order of Succession:* Each movement in kata must be performed in the following order: eyes first, feet next, hands last. These must be done simultaneously, just as the sunshine streams across a room when a door is opened. There must be no gap in the order of succession. This requires precise timing.

Performing warming-up exercises.

3. *Warm-up Exercises:* Warm-up exercises are essential in the training of karate, as in conditioning for sports, and are designed to loosen muscles, joints, and all parts of the body. The warm-up exercises also increase blood circulation and help to prevent the student from being injured because of strained muscles, or unreadiness for speedy movements. Any physical exercises from sports or other martial arts may be added to the warm-up when necessary.

The warm-up exercises begin with extending and contracting the legs, and turning the head several times from left to right, bending it forward and backward, as well as swinging it in a circle. The trunk of the body is bent and stretched forward, backward, and sideward. Jumping makes the body and shoulders relaxed and rhythmical. Finally, several deep breaths complete the exercises. Five minutes are sufficient for the above series of movements.

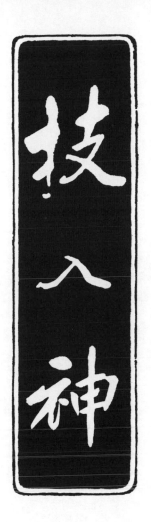

PART TWO

Calligraphy (*overleaf*):
"Practicing karate lengthens one's life span."

IV

Interpretation of the Kata of Matsubayashi-ryu Karate-do

Kata can be described as a systematically organized series of defensive and offensive techniques performed in a sequence against one or more imaginary opponents, and given a symmetrical, linear pattern. Included are the techniques of punching, blocking, striking, and kicking. A careful study of the kata reveals that these exercises are paired units of defensive and offensive techniques. That is, a defensive technique and an offensive technique are combined to form a single unit. Combinations of these techniques, or paired units, in a pattern, are called kata.

The movements of a kata are divided into basic and intermediate. The basic movements are the fundamental defensive and offensive movements of karate and are prerequisites for kata. The intermediate movements serve to connect the basic movements, one to the other, and are frequently used in pre-arranged kumite. Intermediate movements are discussed more fully later in this chapter, while a more detailed explanation of kumite (sparring) follows in Chapter VI (p. 246.)

The intermediate movements are not part of the paired techniques of offense and defense, but are fighting postures that act as links between the paired units. The intermediate movements must not, however, be thought of in a separate context, for they are woven into a kata and are indispensable to it. The intermediate and basic movements combine to produce the vital power of karate.

There exists no perfectly workable theory on how and why the basic and intermediate movements came to be

55

combined in the various kata. Because of the secrecy in which karate had to be practiced and the total reliance on oral tradition, no single well-documented theory on the origins and development of the kata was formulated. There are as many theories concerning the origins and execution of the kata as there are schools of karate. Some have theorized, for example, that the movements of the kata derived from mimicking the protective movements of animals. Others have speculated that the kata grew out of ancient dance forms. Consequently, the manner in which kata should be executed is also open to various interpretations.

Unfortunately, the lack of a comprehensive theory of the movements and how they are executed results in less interest in simple practice of the basic movements of the kata than in the showy intermediate movements employed in kumite. Karate requires endurance and commitment that transcends the mere physical, and the student can begin to appreciate this only after he has so thoroughly mastered the basic movements that they become part of his being.

Because the practice of the basic movements of kata is the focus, and mastery of self is the essence of Matsubayashi-ryu karate-do, I shall try to elucidate the movements of the kata according to my interpretation based on forty years of study. It is not an easy task to explain each movement and its significance, and some must remain unexplained. To give a complete explanation, one would have to be qualified and inspired to such an extent that he could reach the state of enlightened mind capable of recognizing "soundless sound" and "shapeless shape." I do not deem myself the final authority, but my experience with kata has left no doubt that the following is the proper application and interpretation. I offer my theories in the hope that the essence of Okinawan karate will remain intact.

BASIC MOVEMENTS

The basic movements are the fundamental defensive and offensive movements of karate. The karate student must practice these fundamentals thoroughly until they become an instinctive part of his own character. To train the body properly, constant repetition of each movement is required. Only long and extensive training through repetition will enable the student to fuse all of his strength into the movements of kata. Generations of experience have shown that it usually requires three years to learn the basics and seven years to acquire a fundamental proficiency of kata.

Practice of the basic movements enables the student to achieve a natural, beautiful, swift, stable, and powerful performance of kata.˙ From this comes the reflexes and spontaneous movements necessary for defense and offense in actual combat. Thus, mastery of karate-do begins with the basic movements.

The basic movements are largely divided into five categories: *kamaekata* (ready stances); *tachikata* (stances); *semekata* (attacking techniques); *ukekata* (blocking techniques); *kerikata* (kicking techniques).

◆ KAMAEKATA (Ready Stances)

Matsubayashi-ryu karate-do has eighteen kata (forms). Each kata has a given ready stance which begins and ends every performance.

The following are the three types of *kamaekata* (ready stances), and the kata that begin with them. In every case, the shoulders are relaxed and the eyes are fixed straight ahead.

1. Soto-hachiji shizentai-dachi (Open-leg natural stance)

In kata that begin with *soto-hachiji shizentai-dachi,* the feet are separated. The width of the shoulders is taken as the distance between the feet; the toes point out at a 45-degree angle. This stance is found in the following kata:

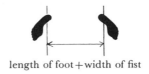

length of foot+width of fist

1

2

3

PINAN I, II, III, IV, V, and GOJUSHIHO. In all of the Pinan kata and Gojushiho, the arms hang straight down naturally. The elbows are relaxed; the fists are placed slightly away from the body, and the distance between them is approximately one and a half fists (Fig. 1).

ROHAI. In Rohai, the arms are placed as above. The hands, however, are open with palms facing each other (Fig. 2).

KUSANKU. In Kusanku, the hands are open with the fingers together. The left palm is placed on the back of the right hand as if the two were joined through the first two knuckles. The thumbs are slightly bent and closed (Fig. 3).

58 CHAPTER IV

4

5

2. Chokuritsu-fudo-dachi (Formal attention stance)

In kata that begin with *chokuritsu-fudo-dachi*, the heels are. together with the toes pointing outward at a 60-degree angle. This stance is found in the following kata:

FUKYUGATA I, II. In the two Fukyugata, the hands are placed as in Kusanku (Fig. 4).

WANKAN. In Wankan, the right fist is placed on the left palm as in the picture (Fig. 5).

6

7

3. Heisoku-dachi (Closed-foot stance)

Here the feet are fully together and point straight ahead. This ready stance is found in the following kata:
NAIHANCHI I, II, III, Passai, Chinto, and Ananku. In these kata, the right fist is covered by the left palm and placed slightly away from the groin (Fig. 6).

WANSHU. In Wanshu, the hands are located approximately one-fist distance away from the chest with the arms forming a horizontal line. The right wrist is straight, its fist covered by the bent palm and fingers of the left hand (Fig. 7).

◆ TACHIKATA (Stances)

Karate-do is a martial art and ultimately can be used in a "kill or be killed" situation. Therefore, the following points must be borne in mind in practicing any stance:

1. Long endurance
2. Stability and balance
3. Flexibility and mobility

These three conditions are fulfilled in *shizentai-dachi* (natural stance), the most characteristic and important stance in Matsubayashi-ryu karate-do. Natural stance is ideal for *tachikata* in karate, and we can find it applied to the other martial arts and sports such as kendo, judo, aikido, boxing and wrestling. Furthermore, these three conditions are essential requirements of the other major Matsubayashi-ryu stances, *jigotai-dachi* (wide open-leg stance) and *zenkutsu-dachi* (front-leg-bent stance), and the trained karateman will recognize these conditions in the remaining stances. However, these three conditions are frequently neglected in the kata exercise and free-style sparring in some schools of karate. Nevertheless, all karate-do devotees must recognize the important role of these principles in karate training.

In all of the *tachikata,* it is essential for the student to master the proper coordination of the particular technique with the twisting motion of the hips. In Japanese, this is called *koshi o ireru,* or "putting in the hip." *Koshi* literally refers to "the small of the back," but the word "hip" is commonly used for a clearer description of the movement.

Following is a practical explanation of *tachikata:*

1. Shizentai-dachi (Natural stance)

Technically, all stances fulfilling the three basic conditions mentioned above can be called natural stances. However, I refer to two particularly as *shizentai-dachi* (natural stance), because they correspond directly to the natural physical movements employed in our daily life when we stand or walk. By calling these natural stances, I wish to draw the student's attention to the natural spacing and distances taken from these everyday movements, which are frequently overlooked in the free-style sparring techniques popular today.

1   2   3

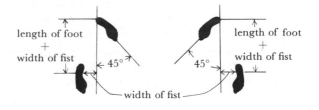

length of foot + width of fist

length of foot + width of fist   45°

length of foot + width of fist   45°

width of fist

1. SOTO-HACHIJI SHIZENTAI-DACHI (Open-leg natural stance)

As explained previously in the section under *kamaekata* (ready stances), the distance between the feet is the same as the width of the shoulders. This is the foot position employed most naturally and normally in daily life (Fig. 1).

2. MIGI-ASHI-MAE SHIZENTAI-DACHI (Right-foot-front natural stance) and HIDARI-ASHI-MAE SHIZENTAI-DACHI (Left-foot-front natural stance)

In both stances, the distance between the feet is the same as when taking a step forward. As shown in the diagram, there is about one foot-width or fist-width between the heels, and the same distance from the toe of the back foot to the heel of the front foot. The back foot points outward at a 45-degree angle (Figs. 2, 3).

62   CHAPTER IV

4   5

60°

2. Jun shizentai-dachi (Quasi-natural stance)

Compared to the other stances the following stances are somewhat similar to *shizentai-dachi*. However, strictly speaking, they do not completely fulfill the three basic conditions as shizentai-dachi. Therefore, they are classified as quasi-natural stances.

1. CHOKURITSU-FUDO-DACHI (Formal attention stance)
As explained previously in the section under *kamaekata,* the heels are together with the toes pointing outward at a 60-degree angle, and the shoulders are relaxed (Fig. 4).

2. HEISOKU-DACHI (Closed-foot stance)
This stance has also been explained previously in the section under *kamaekata*; that is, the feet are fully together and point straight ahead, and the shoulders are relaxed (Fig. 5).

6 (first view)   6 (second view)

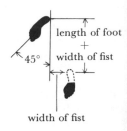

length of foot
+
width of fist

45°

width of fist

3. NEKOASHI-DACHI (Cat stance)

Nekoashi-dachi as well as *shizentai-dachi* has been regarded as one of the most important stances in kata of each of Shuri-te, Naha-te, and Tomari-te. The martial arts find *nekoashi-dachi* the most useful or effective technique to be emphasized in practice, though it seems to be rather neglected in the karate often observed in the United States and mainland Japan.

Nekoashi-dachi is formed from a *shizentai-dachi* stance by assuming balance with the back leg, which must be bent and which carries all the weight. The front foot lightly touches the floor and the angle of the bent knee is deepened until there is a vertical line between the knee and the big toe (Fig. 6).

Nekoashi-dachi is practiced by quickly moving forward and backwards in a straight line, or from side to side. In actual fighting, this stance is most advantageous for attacking an opponent's side. I want to emphasize that although *nekoashi-dachi* appears like a defensive stance, it is equally effective for offensive techniques. In this stance activity lives with inactivity, or in Miyamoto Musashi's words, "*Seichu do ari, dochu sei ari.*" (In stillness there is activity, in activity there is stillness).

7   8   9

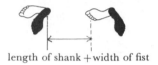

length of shank + width of fist

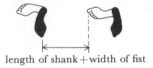

length of shank + width of fist

3. Jigotai-dachi (Wide open-leg stance)

Jigotai-dachi is an effective stance for blocking attacks coming from the front or sides, when it is impossible to shift one's self. This stance is formed by taking a balanced stance with the legs (Fig. 7). The hips are lowered with the center of gravity, and the groin area is drawn in protectively. The correct distance between the legs is found by the following procedure as shown in the picture (Fig. 8). Bend over, one knee touching the floor. Make sure the heel of that foot is sticking straight up, perpendicular to the floor. Place the other foot in line with the knee, a width of one fist between them. Stand up without moving the feet from their spots on the floor, but allowing them to pivot so that the toes will point outwards to the front at a 45-degree angle.

4. Naihanchi-dachi (Straddle-leg stance)

This stance is formed in the exact manner as *jigotai-dachi* or wide open-leg stance except that the feet must be parallel to each other (Fig. 9).

10 (first view)　　　　10 (second view)　　　　11

length of shank
+
width of fist

width of fist

length of shank
+
width of fist

45°

45°

5. Zenkutsu-dachi (Front-leg-bent stance)

Zenkutsu-dachi is a desperate stance for managing a way out of difficulties at the risk of one's life, especially when driven to a corner, or with one's back to a wall. It is formed by stretching the back leg fully straight and by bending the front until its knee makes a vertical line with its toe. The same distance between the feet is taken as explained in *jigotai-dachi*. The hips must be twisted fully front when executing a defensive or offensive movement with the arms (Fig. 10).

6. Naname zenkutsu-dachi (Slanted front-leg-bent stance)

From *jigotai-dachi* or wide open-leg stance, we can form *naname zenkutsu-dachi* by simply straightening one leg, and allowing the foot of that leg to pivot enough to become parallel with the other foot. This stance is found in Wankan and Ananku (Fig. 11).

12   13 (first view)   13 (second view)

7. Kokutsu-dachi (Back-leg-bent stance)

This stance is formed by extending the front leg straight, while bending and balancing with the back leg. The same distance between the legs is taken as in *jigotai-dachi*. This defensive stance is easily assumed to block an attack when one is already in the *zenkutsu-dachi* (Fig. 12).

8. Kosa-dachi (Cross-leg stance)

Kosa-dachi is formed by taking balance on one leg, which is slightly bent. The other leg crosses behind the balancing leg, and the toes are placed on the floor in direct line with the heel of the balancing foot. The legs are pressed together. This stance is often used when preparing to kick without being noticed by the opponent (Fig. 13).

KATA INTERPRETATION: TACHIKATA **67**

14

15 (a)

15 (b)

9. Ippon-ashi-dachi (One-leg stance)

This stance is a blocking posture as shown in the picture. The thigh and foot of the raised leg are parallel to the floor and the body is erect (Fig. 14).

10. Iaigoshi-dachi (Kneeling stance)

In Chinto kata, this stance is taken to give a vital blow to the opponent lying down. However, this stance may be used against many kinds of attacks. It is extremely effective when one is already in Japanese *seiza* (formal sitting position) (Figs. 15 a, b).

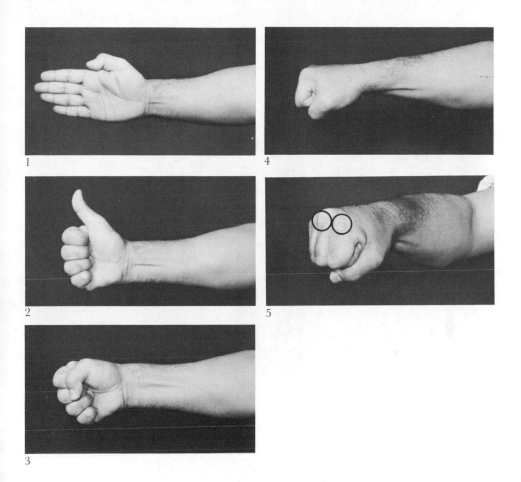

1   4

2   5

3

◆ SEMEKATA (Attacking Techniques)

Karate-do employs every part of the body, toughened by long and hard training for self-defense. Although practically every part of the body can be a vital weapon, the most vital blows can be produced with fists, hands, elbows, and the feet.

1. Seiken waza (Fist technique)

Seiken is formed by bending the fingers at the second joints, clenching them tightly into the palm, and pressing both the forefinger and the middle finger with the thumb as shown in the picture. The wrist must be kept straight; it is an extension of the right angle formed between the top and front of the fist (Figs. 1–5).

6

7

The knuckles of the forefinger and the middle finger are toughened by striking *makiwara*.

The various kinds of *seiken* and the kata in which they are used are as follows:

1. JODAN-ZUKI (Upper punch)
Fukyugata I, II, and Pinan II (Fig. 6).

2. CHUDAN-ZUKI (Middle punch)
Fukyugata I and most other kata (Fig. 7).

3. GEDAN-ZUKI (Lower punch)
Rohai, Wanshu, Passai, and Chinto (Figs. 8, 9).

4. KAKU-ZUKI (Square punch)
Naihanchi I, II, III, and Pinan V (Figs. 10, 11).

5. TOMOE-ZUKI (Circular block and punch)
This is used with *zenkutsu-dachi* or *nekoashi-dachi* to deliver a blow to the chest and abdomen simultaneously. Fukyugata II, Rohai, and Passai (Figs. 12, 13).

14

15 (a)

15 (b)

6. SAYU-ZUKI (Double side punch)

This is formed by extending both arms straight to each side. Wankan and Chinto (Fig. 14).

7. KAKUSHI-ZUKI (Hidden fist punch)

The fist is placed on the lower part of the back, and the punch is delivered from there. Wanshu (Figs. 15 a, b).

8. OI-ZUKI (Chasing punch)

This is used in conjunction with *jigotai-dachi* or wide open-leg stance to deliver a blow to the opponent's chest by extending the fist sideward. Pinan III, Passai, Chinto, Gojushiho, and Kusanku (Fig. 16).

9. WARI-UKE-ZUKI (Split-block punch)

This is formed by executing simultaneously an upper block and an upper punch. Chinto (Fig. 17).

10. MOROTE-ZUKI (Augmented-side punch)

This is formed similarly to *oi-zuki* or chasing punch with one of the hands serving to accelerate the force of the other while staying parallel to it. Naihanchi I and Kusanku (Fig. 18).

16

17 (first view)

17 (second view)

18

KATA INTERPRETATION: SEMEKATA **73**

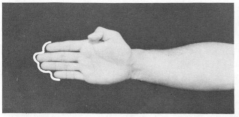

19

22

20

21

23

2. Yubi waza (Finger technique)

In place of a fist, the extended fingers are tightened together and used as a spear or a beak. Some *yubi waza* and their use in kata are as follows:

1. NUKITE-ZUKI (Spear-hand thrust)

This technique is formed with the fingers extended and tightened together and is used to thrust at the eyes, solar plexus or ribs. Pinan I, III, Gojushiho, and Kusanku (Figs. 19, 20).

2. MOROTE-NUKI-ZUKI (Double spear-hand thrust)

Both hands are used as in *nukite-zuki* above. Gojushiho (Fig. 21).

3. SHI-ZUKI (Beak thrust)

This is formed by tightening the fingers and thumb closely in the shape of a bird's beak as shown in the pictures. Gojushiho (Figs. 22, 23).

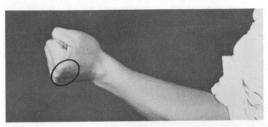

24

25   26

3. Uchi waza (Striking technique)

As striking techniques, there are uses of the fists called *uraken* (backfist) and *kentsui* (hammer fist), which are regarded as variants of *seiken*, or fist punch, as well as uses of the hands called *shuto* (knife-hand) and *haito* (reverse knife-hand). These are explained in detail as follows:

1. URAKEN-UCHI (Backfist strike)

The fist is formed as in *seiken*. It is used to strike the face or chest of an opponent by making use of the snap of the fore-arm when one is too closely approached to use *seiken* or fist punch. When executing this technique, it is important to keep the fist and arm tight, while allowing the wrist to flex, adding to the snapping effect of the blow. Pinan III, IV, Passai, Naihanchi I, II, III, and Gojushiho (Figs. 24–26).

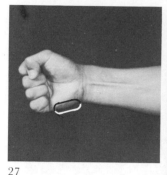

27

28

29

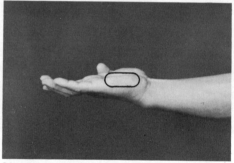

30

2. KENTSUI-UCHI (Hammer-fist strike)

The fist is formed the same way as in *seiken*, but the side is used to block the opponent's hand or arm by making a snapping motion with the forearm as if using a hammer. Pinan II and Naihanchi III (Figs. 27–29).

3. SHUTO-UCHI (Knife-hand strike)

This is formed by stretching the four fingers, joined tightly, and pressing the thumb, bent at the first joint, to the root of the forefinger (Fig. 30).

This technique can be used in several ways, three of which follow:

31

32

33

(a) *Kyobu shuto-uchi* (Chest knife-hand strike). This strike is used to slash the opponent's neck as in Fukyugata II (Fig. 31).

(b) *Kyobu morote shuto-uchi* (Chest double knife-hand strike). This strike is used to attack both of the opponent's collarbones simultaneously. Chinto (Fig. 32).

(c) *Kyobu-soete shuto-uchi* (Chest augmented knife-hand strike). Both hands, with palms facing each other, are used as knife-hand to attack ribs or side. Chinto (Fig. 33).

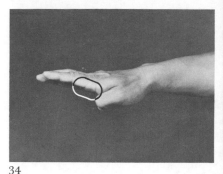

34

35

4. HAITO-UCHI (Reverse knife-hand strike)

This technique is formed the same way as in *shuto-uchi* (Fig. 34). However, the opposite side of the hand, that is, the ridge of the hand that lies in front of the thumb, is used to block and strike the opponent's forearm, neck or fist. Naihanchi I (Fig. 35). It can be noted that the knife-hand striking techniques mentioned above could also be used or interpreted as blocking techniques.

4. Ate waza (Smashing technique)

The smashing techniques employ the elbows, knees, and heels of the palms to deliver powerful, vital blows to such parts of the body as the chest, ribs, face, and legs.

1. HIJI-ATE (Elbow smash)

This is employed to deliver a powerful blow to the chest, ribs, and chin or jaw when one is too closely approached or suddenly hugged by an opponent. *Hiji-ate* is generally applied with the fist closed, but could also be used with the hand open (Fig. 36). The four types of *hiji-ate* are seen in the following Matsubayashi-ryu kata:

(a) *Tate hiji-ate* (Upward elbow smash). Fukyugata II and Gojushiho (Fig. 37).

(b) *Yoko hiji-ate* (Forward elbow smash). Pinan IV, V, Naihanchi, Passai, and Kusanku (Fig. 38).

(c) *Ushiro hiji-ate* (Backward elbow smash). Pinan III (Fig. 39).

(d) *Sasae hiji-ate* (Supported elbow smash). Naihanchi II (Fig. 40).

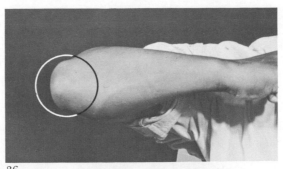

36

37

38

39

40

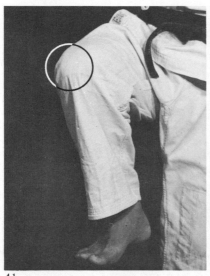

41   42

2. Hɪᴢᴀ-ᴀᴛᴇ (Knee smash)

This is used to deliver a vital blow to the groin, abdomen or chest of an opponent when closely approached or tackled. This technique is most effective if thoroughly practiced until it becomes a spontaneous reflex. Pinan IV (Figs. 41, 42).

3. Sʜᴏᴛᴇɪ-ᴀᴛᴇ (Palm-heel smash)

This is formed by opening the hand and bending the wrist backward until the bottom or heel of the palm is tensed and hardened; it is used to give a blow to the chin, groin, chest, or kicking leg of an opponent (Fig. 43).

(a) *Jodan shotei-ate* (Upper palm-heel smash). This technique is used to strike the chin upward. Passai (Fig. 44).

(b) *Chudan shotei-ate* (Middle palm-heel smash). This is used to block and strike the side of the trunk. Wanshu (Fig. 45).

(c) *Gedan shotei-ate* (Lower palm-heel smash). This is used with *zenkutsu-dachi* to smash the groin or kicking leg of the opponent. Rohai and Wanshu (Figs. 46, 47).

(d) *Tomoe shotei-ate* (Circular palm-heel smash). This is used to block a punching attack from the front and simultaneously smash the solar plexus and abdomen. Kusanku (Fig. 48).

43

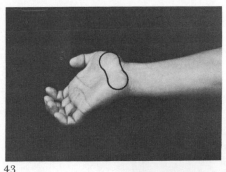

44   45

46   47   48

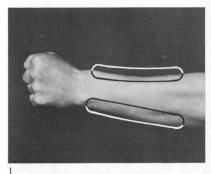

1

2 (a)

2 (b)

◆ UKEKATA (Blocking Techniques)

The ultimate goal of all martial arts is to defeat the enemy without fighting back. This notion is intimately connected with the essence of karate-do and is expressed as the philosophy of karate in the proverb, *karate ni sente nashi* (there is no first attack in karate, or karate begins only with the defensive form.) There are always some persons around who do violence to good citizens; the blocking techniques have been developed to meet such violence.

What follows is a practical explanation of *ukekata:*

1. Seiken-ude-uke (Forearm block)

In all of the *seiken-ude-uke* blocks which follow, both sides of the forearm, in conjunction with a fist, are used in various ways to block attacks (Fig. 1). This is a most effective technique and is frequently used in kata as well as free-style sparring.

1. JODAN UKE (Upper block)

This block is formed by raising the forearm to the height of the forehead. The distance between the wrist and the forehead is one fist and the blocking arm forms a 45-degree angle. Fukyugata I, II, and Pinan I, II (Figs. 2 a, b).

3 (a)   3 (b)

4   5

2. CHUDAN SOTO-UKE (Middle outward block)

This block is formed by bending the arm at approximately a 90-degree angle. The wrist is on the same line as the shoulders. The muscles under the arm (latissimus dorsi, teres major) are tensed when the force is focused on contact. Fukyugata II and most other kata (Figs. 3 a, b).

3. CHUDAN YOKO-UKE (Middle sideward block)

This is the same as *chudan soto-uke*, except that it is executed to the side. Naihanchi II, III, and Wanshu (Fig. 4).

4. CHUDAN UCHI-UKE (Middle inner block)

This is formed as in *chudan soto-uke*; however, it blocks toward the inside by a snapped motion of the forearm. Naihanchi I, II, Chinto, and Kusanku (Fig. 5).

6 (first view)   6 (second view)   7

5. GEDAN UKE (Lower block)

This is used to block kicks aimed at the lower part of the body. It is seen in many kata, including Fukyugata I and II (Fig. 6).

6. GEDAN YOKO-BARAI-UKE (Lower sideward block)

This sideward block is used in conjunction with *jigotai-dachi* to block a kick. Fukyugata II, Naihanchi I, and Kusanku (Fig. 7).

7. SASAE-UKE (Supported forearm block)

The fist of the blocking arm is supported by the open hand of the other arm. Naihanchi II and Passai (Fig. 8).

8. SAYU-BARAI-UKE (Double lower side block)

This block is used to block kicks coming from both sides at once. Wanshu and Ananku (Fig. 9).

9. JODAN WARI-UKE (Upper split block)

This block employs both fists which are used as in *jodan uke*. There is a fist's width or less between the two fists. Passai, Chinto, and Gojushiho (Fig. 10).

10. CHUDAN WARI-UKE (Middle split block)

This block is formed by using *chudan soto-uke* with both forearms. Pinan V, Ananku, and Chinto (Figs. 11, 12).

8

9

10 (first view)

10 (second view)

12

11

13   14

15 (first view)   15 (second view)

11. JODAN KOSA-UKE (Upper cross block)

Both arms form *jodan uke* with the wrists crossed one fist's distance from the forehead (Fig. 13).

12. GEDAN KOSA-UKE (Lower cross block)

This is formed by blocking downward with the forearm and crossing it with the right fist. Pinan IV, V, and Chinto (Fig. 14).

13. MOROTE SOE-UKE (Augmented forearm block)

This mid-region outward moving block is formed by using *chudan soto-uke* and augmenting the movement with the other arm. Pinan I, IV, and V (Figs. 15).

16

17

18

14. CHUDAN SOTO-MAWASHI-UKE (Middle sideward round block)

This is formed in the same way as in *chudan yoko-uke*, except that the fist is turned outwards, as in the picture. Naihanchi I and II (Fig. 16).

15. MOROTE-BARAI-UKE (Augmented lower block)

This is formed by executing *gedan uke* with one arm, while simultaneously augmenting it by executing *chudan soto-uke* with the other arm. Pinan III, Naihanchi I, II, III, and Passai (Figs. 17, 18).

19   20

21

16. HAZUSHI-UKE (Removing block)

This is formed by raising the forearms quickly to chest height, with forearms level, fists about one fist-width apart, and one fist-width from the chest. Naihanchi II and Gojushiho (Figs. 19, 20).

17. OTOSHI-UKE (Dropping downward block)

The arm is dropped down from the height of the ear to block a kicking leg. Pinan V and Passai (Fig. 21).

22 (a)

22 (b)

22 (c)

2. Shuto- and haito-uke (Knife-hand and reverse knife-hand blocks)

The knife-hand and reverse knife-hand have already been shown in *uchi waza* or striking technique:

1. CHUDAN SOTO-SHUTO-UKE (Middle outward knife-hand block)

Chudan soto-shuto-uke is most frequently used for blocking, but it is very difficult for beginners to manage properly (Figs. 22a, b, c). The arm is bent at a 90-degree angle, with the wrist in line with the shoulder; the outer or blocking edge of the knife-hand twists from the opposite shoulder to its contact position. The other hand is used to augment the power and acts to guard the solar plexus area. This block is seen in many kata including Pinan I and IV. The skillful use of this technique requires constant practice.

23 (a)   23 (b)   24

2. JODAN UCHI-SHUTO-UKE (Upper inner knife-hand block)

Here the knife-hand is slashed from ear height forward to block a punch. Usually delivered from *nekoashi-dachi* stance. Pinan IV, Passai, and Kusanku (Figs. 23 a, b, 24).

3. CHUDAN YOKO-SHUTO-UKE (Middle sideward knife-hand block)

This is used to block a punch to the side of the face. Naihanchi II and III (Fig. 25).

4. GEDAN SHUTO-UKE (Lower knife-hand block)

In this block, the knife-hand twists from the opposite shoulder to its contact position straight down and about six inches or one hand-span above the front knee. The other knife-hand augments the power as both hands form the same plane; it also guards the groin area. It is used to block a kick aimed at the abdomen. Pinan II (Figs. 26a, b).

5. GEDAN SHUTO YOKO-BARAI-UKE (Lower sideward knife-hand slashing block)

This is used in conjunction with *jigotai-dachi*. The blocking hand moves as in *gedan yoko-barai-uke*; the other knife-hand is used to augment the power as both hands form the same plane. Rohai (Fig. 27).

6. CHUDAN HASAMI-UKE (Middle scissors block)

This block is formed by crossing the right knife-hand over the left knife-hand in front of the face at nose height. The backs of the hands face each other. The crossed knife-hands can then be used to grab and twist the opponent's hand or arm, making it easy to attack him with the other hand. Pinan V, Ananku, and Chinto (Fig. 28).

25

27   26 (a)

26 (b)

28

29 (a)   29 (b)

29 (c)   29 (d)

7. MAKITE-UKE (Winding knife-hand block)

This block is difficult to describe because it moves in two stages: In the first stage, the knife-hand moves from the bottom to the top of a half circle. Its contact point is inside of the forearm. The hand is now forming reverse knife-hand. The forearm rests on the other hand which supports this blocking forearm. The elbow is at a 90-degree angle. In step II, the reverse knife-hand turns over to grab the opponent and pull him while the other hand punches him. Rohai, Wankan, Wanshu, and Passai (Figs. 29 a, b, c, d).

8. MAGETORI-BARAI-UKE (Rising upward both-hand knife block)

Both knife-hands are swept away above the forehead to remove the hands of the opponent who is holding you by the hair. Chinto (Figs. 30a, b).

30 (a)

30 (b)

31

32

33

9. TORITE-UKE (Grasping-hand block)

Torite is used to block and pull the opponent's arm so that you can punch him with the other hand. Rohai, Wanshu, Gojushiho, and Chinto (Fig. 31).

10. SAGURITE-UKE (Searching-hand block)

This is seen in the last part of Passai kata and was originally used to search for the opponent at close range in the dark. Used only in Passai (Fig. 32).

11. GEDAN HAITO-YOKO-UKE (Lower sideward reverse knife-hand block)

This is formed in the same manner as *gedan shuto yoko-barai-uke* (lower sideward knife-hand slashing block), except that the blocking hand is turned palm upwards to form the reverse knife-hand block. Gojushiho (Fig. 33).

34 (first view)   34 (second view)   35

36   37

3. Shotei-uke (Palm-heel block)

The heel of the palm is called *shotei,* which was previously described in the section on *ate waza* or smashing technique (p. 80).

1. CHUDAN SHOTEI-UKE (Middle palm-heel block)
Here the heel of the palm blocks a punch by striking underneath the opponent's forearm. This block can be easily changed into a punch. Kusanku (Figs. 34, 35).

2. GEDAN SHOTEI-UKE (Lower palm-heel block)
This term is used to describe all palm-heel blocks to the lower region. Rohai, Wanshu, and Kusanku (Figs. 36, 37).

38 (a)   38 (b)

39 (a)   39 (b)   39 (c)

4. Hiji-uke (Elbow block)

Hiji-uke is formed by placing both forefists on the waist, and is used to block an attack to the chest. It changes into *uraken-uchi* or backfist strike immediately after blocking with the elbow. Pinan III and Chinto (Figs. 38a, b).

5. Hangetsu-barai-uke (Half-moon foot block)

This block is formed by swinging the back leg of *zenkutsu-dachi* (front-leg-bent stance) or *nekoashi-dachi* (cat stance) in a half circle to remove the opponent's hand when one's own hand has been grabbed. At the moment of contact, the foot can turn and change into a downward side kick. Due to the crescent-shaped movement of the blocking foot, it is called half-moon foot block. Rohai, Passai, and Kusanku (Figs. 39a, b, c).

◆ KERIKATA (Kicking Techniques)

In karate-do, kicking techniques are very powerful only when they are skillfully used with stability and proper balance. The student should realize, however, that kicking techniques require prudence and caution, since any disturbance of his kicking leg by the opponent could easily upset his equilibrium or open him up to an attack.

Kicks should be aimed at the lower part of the body, the sides of the trunk or the solar plexus. The kicking leg must be pulled back as soon as possible, keeping the body balanced with the axis leg. However, there is a tendency in free-style sparring, or in competition, frequently to use kicking techniques to aim at the face or upper part of the body, without careful attention that the body's balance be stabilized. This easy use of kicking may be allowable from the viewpoint of sports but not in a "life or death" situation which is the premise of a martial art.

To obviate the danger of being tripped, the kicking techniques must be used only when the opponent is close enough, or when caught by the hand or arm. For this reason, the most effective kicks in Matsubayashi-ryu karate-do are as follows:

1. Kyobu-geri (Chest kick)
Ball of the foot, *josokutei*, is used to kick the opponent's chest and solar plexus. Pinan IV and Kusanku (Figs. 1, 2).

2. Fukubu-geri (Abdomen kick)
Tips of toes, *tsumasaki*, are used to kick the lower region of the body. This was Arakaki's speciality. Fukyugata II, Pinan I, IV, Ananku, Gojushiho, and Chinto (Figs. 3, 4).

3. Kinteki-geri (Groin kick)
Instep of the foot, *sokko*, is used to kick the groin or strike the side of the legs. Chinto (Figs. 5, 6).

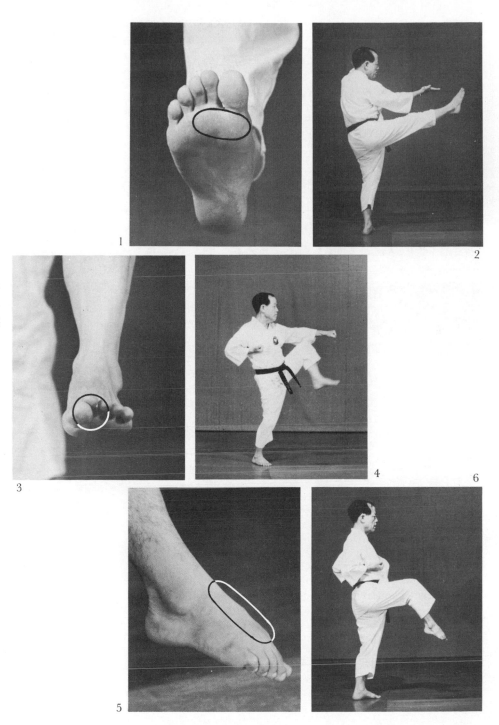

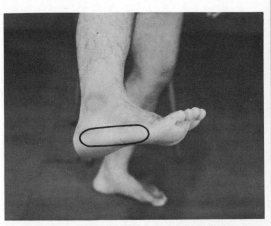

7

8

9 (a)

9 (b)

9 (c)

4. Sokuto-geri (Foot-edge kick)

Foot-edge, *sokuto,* is very powerful when used to strike the opponent's knees, legs, abdomen and ribs. Foot-edge kick is most effective when used with *torite* block (pulling the opponent toward you). Passai (Figs. 7, 8).

5. Nidan-geri (Flying front kick)

Nidan-geri is a desperate kicking technique for managing a way out of difficulties in a risk situation, especially when driven to a corner or dead end (Figs. 9a, b, c).

INTERMEDIATE MOVEMENTS

The intermediate movements, as I mentioned earlier in this chapter, are integrated into the kata as links between the paired units of the basic movements. The integration of the intermediate movements was accomplished over the centuries by the great masters of Okinawan karate. These masters spent their lives searching for movements that were both physiologically sound and effective as defensive and offensive techniques. When they found those movements that were physically logical, physiologically correct, and offensively and defensively workable, they dovetailed them into kata. The centuries of work by the masters to arrange the rhythmical execution of the kata and to give it a linear, symmetrical direction resulted in the intermediate movements as we know them today.

That the intermediate movements are physiologically sound has been proven by long experience. When practiced correctly, these movements elicit a person's maximum physical capabilities and are never detrimental to the body's physical development. The intermediate movements also act as aids to the execution of the kata. For example, the intermediate movements serve to readjust breathing; gasping for breath and exhaustion during practice are eased by these movements.

The physical logic of the intermediate movements is apparent when they are compared to other forms of physical endeavor, such as dance and sports. One of the most important functions of the intermediate movements is that of "positional coincidence"; they cause the final position of the kata to coincide with the initial position. The kata begins at one point and ends at the same point so that symmetry of position, as well as movement, is upheld. This positional coincidence for the beginning and end of kata is stressed in both Shuri-te and Tomari-te. It can also be observed in Okinawan folk dances, and the greatest Okinawan folk musicians accept this theory of positional coincidence. Needless to say, the Okinawan folk dance is different in function from karate, but both of them have many common characteristics in the movement of feet and hands. The theory of positional coincidence is also supported by the principles of physical training. Well-balanced movements in symmetry are essential to any exercise or sport.

1   2   3

Along with the physical reasons for the integration of the intermediate movements into kata, the masters developed these movements because their rhythm helps one to be in a state of *zanshin*. *Zanshin* is the state of mind where one is able to proceed from the end of one movement to the next movement freely. It literally means being absolutely attentive to the next move right after the previous move. In *zanshin* the mind focuses completely on the body's movements. To be distracted by another's moves in a fighting situation is to lose *zanshin;* to stop one's mind from flowing from move to move while practicing is to lose *zanshin*.

The fighting postures make the movements of the kata flow. This flow aids the mind to concentrate fully on the movements to such an extent that the person "becomes the movement." Being at one with the movement so that no outside force can interrupt this oneness is the state of *zanshin*.

I find it most remarkable and admirable that a system as refined and complex as kata could be developed by the ancients. The rhythmic, symmetrical combination of physically logical and supremely powerful movements with *zanshin* has made a system that for all intents and purposes is classic, transcending the ages. The system of kata with all its facets is still workable today, and serves to enhance the character and dignity of those who practice it.

All of the Matsubayashi-ryu kata can be logically interpreted and analyzed if one keeps in mind my original premise that the intermediate movements are fighting postures or ready stances that serve as conjunctive move-

4   5   6

ments. Misinterpretation of the significance of the kata results if one replaces the simple and non-spectacular formal exercises with showy free-style sparring.

The following are some intermediate movements I regard as fighting postures:

1. SUIRAKAN NO KAMAE (Drunkard fighting posture) in Passai and Gojushiho. There is an appearance of drunkenness, of defenselessness and unwillingness to fight, but the hands or elbows could be dropped downward quickly in case of an attack (Fig. 1).

2. RYU-NO-SHITA NO KAMAE (Dragon-tongue fighting posture) in Kusanku. The hands are ready to defend quickly or counterattack (Fig. 2).

3. SAGURITE NO KAMAE (Searching-hand fighting posture) in Passai. This movement was designed to minimize an opponent's chance to launch a successful attack in the dark (Fig. 3).

4. HOTOKE-GAMAE (Buddha-hand fighting posture) in Passai and Pinan V. The raised fist could easily be launched as a counterattack or a blocking weapon (Fig. 4).

5. TENSHIN NO KAMAE (Body-shifting fighting posture) in Pinan V. This one is a *tenshin* or sideward movement, allowing the opponent's attack or rush to pass by (Fig. 5).

6. URA-GAMAE (Cheating fighting-posture) in Kusanku. By pivoting and dropping the body, one may foil an attack from behind by quickly removing an opponent's target, thus "cheating" him of his intention to strike (Fig. 6).

When interpreting the kata, the method of breathing must also be explained. There is no artificial training for breathing in kata practice. One has only to recognize that basically a defensive technique is executed with inhalation, whereas an offensive technique is executed with exhalation. Kata can then be seen as a series of unitary techniques of defense and offense forming a single unit with an accompanying set of breathing units. In other words, kata is a well-organized series of movement techniques whose single components can be considered in principle to be a defensive technique with inhalation followed by an offensive technique with exhalation.

Because of the unitary aspect of kata, the seemingly isolated technique is actually followed by either inhalation or exhalation, depending on the deletion of the paired counterpart (Pinan Shodan is a good example since it ends with an upper block technique, deleting the paired counterpart which might logically follow a punch, or some other offensive technique). In this case the offensive technique (the punch) is replaced by exhalation in the return to the original starting position.

Learning kata thoroughly is absolutely crucial. Karate training should center on kata. By making kata central to training, one can pursue karate-do not only as budo but as a way of life. The beauty and spirit of kata offers much to those who practice it. Students of karate-do should be determined to set kata at the heart and center of karate-do and practice kumite as supplementary training.

V

Sequential Movements
of the Eighteen Kata

It is believed that there once existed thirty kata in Shuri-te and Tomari-te, but only eighteen have been preserved in Matsubayashi-ryu karate-do; sixteen were inherited from Choki Motobu, Chotoku Kyan, and Ankichi Arakaki, and two (Fukyugata I and II) were later added.

Students will be permitted to apply for black belt rank after rigorously training in these forms for approximately three years:

1.	Fukyugata I	10.	Naihanchi Sandan
2.	Fukyugata II	11.	Ananku
3.	Pinan Shodan	12.	Wankan
4.	Pinan Nidan	13.	Rohai
5.	Pinan Sandan	14.	Wanshu
6.	Pinan Yondan	15.	Passai
7.	Pinan Godan	16.	Gojushiho
8.	Naihanchi Shodan	17.	Chinto
9.	Naihanchi Nidan	18.	Kusanku

The sequential movements of the above eighteen kata are described on the following pages.

Fukyugata I

1   2

普
及
形

FUKYUGATA I, II

Two Fukyugata commonly practiced today were composed by Shoshin Nagamine, the originator of Matsubayashi-ryu karate, and Chojun Miyagi, the originator of Goju-ryu karate, because the kata of the Shuri and Naha schools had been too difficult for beginners. In 1940, two of the compositions were authorized to be the formal basic kata by the special committee of Okinawa karate-do organized and summoned by Gen Hayakawa, then governor of Okinawa Prefecture.

3

4

5

3–4

5–6

7–8

6

7

8

9

10

11

11-12

15-16

15

16 (first view) kiai

16 (second view)

12 13 14

13–14

17 18 19 (first view)

19 (second view) 20 21

19-20 21-22

25 26

22   23   24

23–24

Fukyugata II   1   2

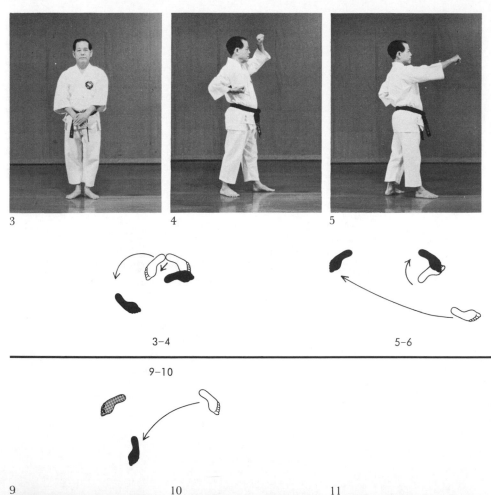

3   4   5

3–4   5–6

9–10

9   10   11

6

7

8

6-7

8-9

12 kiai

13

14

15　　　　　　　　16 (first view)　　　　16 (second view)

15–16　　　　　　　　　　　　　　　16–17

21–22

20　　　　　　　　21　　　　　　　　22 (first view)

17

18

19

22–23

22 (second view)

23

24

25 26 27

31–32

31 32 33

114 CHAPTER V

28

29

30

27-28

34

1   2   3

Pinan I (Shodan)

2-3

PINAN I–V (Shodan–Godan)

Pinan Shodan to Godan were composed in 1907 by Anko Itosu who was born in 1830. They were originally intended for high school students. The name of this kata must be pronounced *pinan*, not *heian*, as it often is in mainland Japan.

4

5

6

3–4

6–7

9–10

7

8

9

7

8

9

10 (first view)　　　　10 (second view)　　　　11 (first view)

14　　　　　　　　15 kiai　　　　　　　16

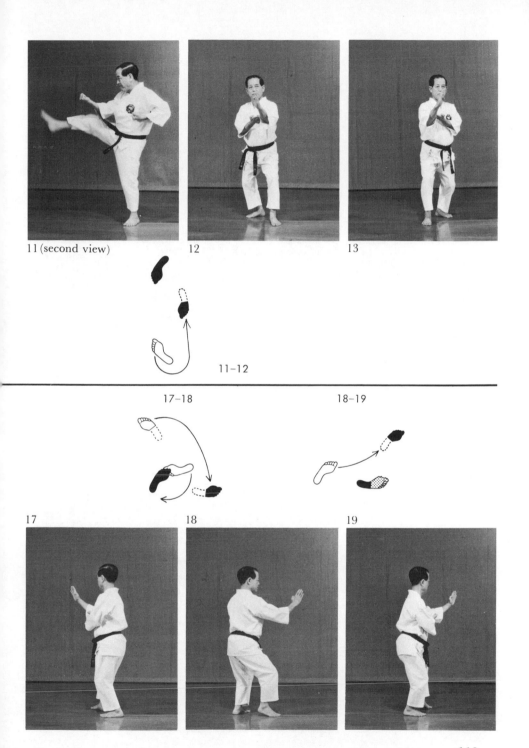

11 (second view) 12 13

11–12

17–18 18–19

17 18 19

20 (first view)　　　20 (second view)　　　21

19–20

27–28

25　　　　　　　　26　　　　　　　　27

22   23   24

28   29   30

29-30

31

32

33

31-32

3-4

Pinan II (Nidan)

1

2

3

34

5-6   6-7

4   5   6

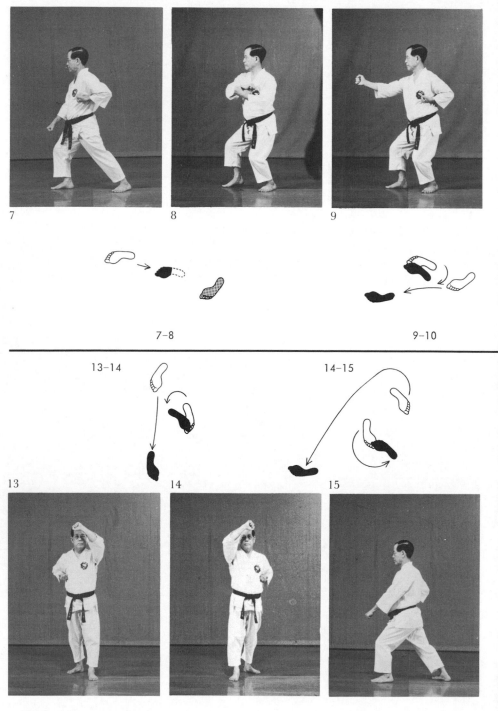

7   8   9

7–8   9–10

13–14   14–15

13   14   15

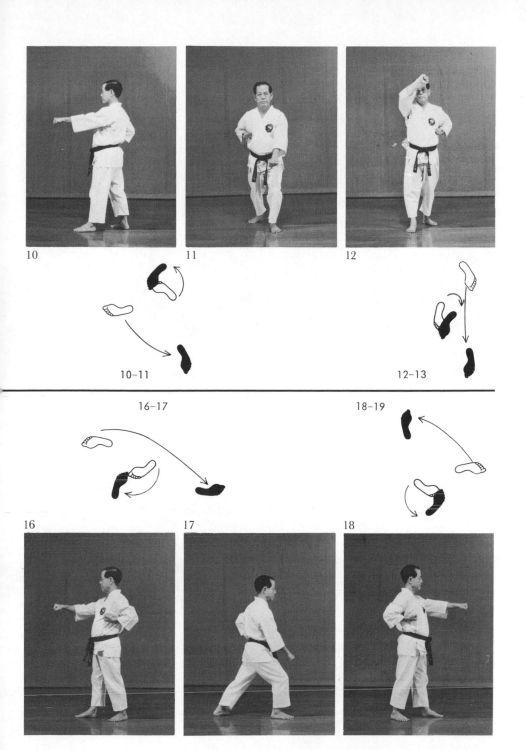

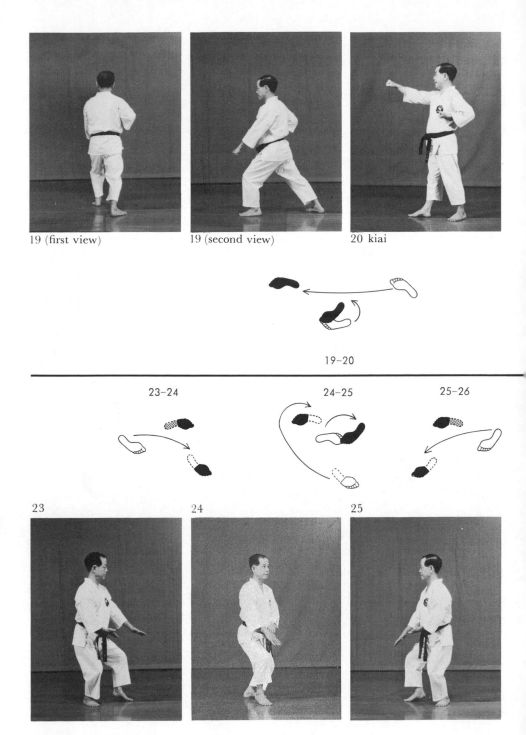

19 (first view) 19 (second view) 20 kiai

19–20

23–24 24–25 25–26

23 24 25

21

22 (first view)

22 (second view)

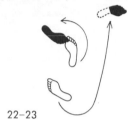

21–22

22–23

26–27

26

27

28

29

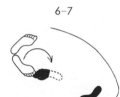

6-7

4   5   6

128 CHAPTER V

1

2

3

3-4

9-10

7

8

9

10   11   12

16–17

16 kiai   17   18 (first view)

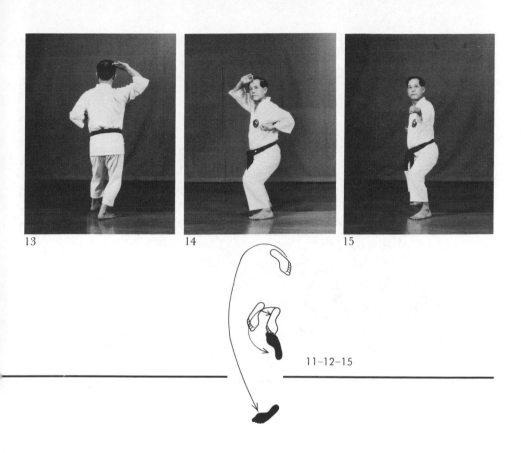

13 14 15

11–12–15

18 (second view) 19 20

21   22   23

21-22

27   28   29

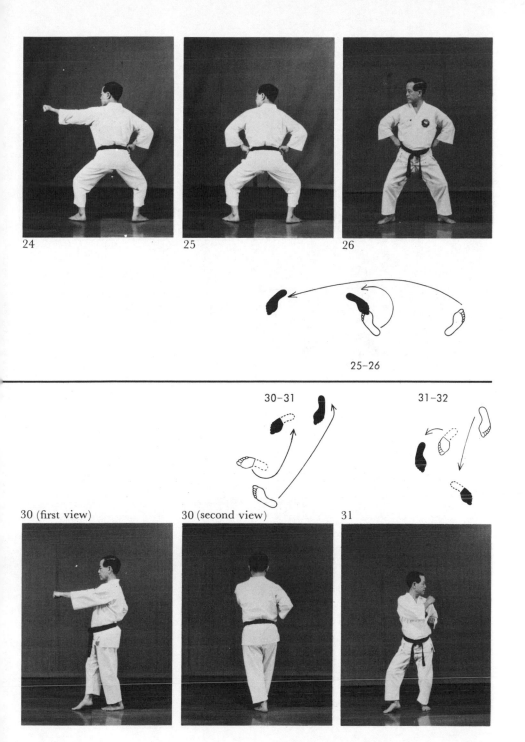

24

25

26

25–26

30–31

31–32

30 (first view)

30 (second view)

31

32

33

34

32-33

3-4

Pinan IV (Yondan)

1

2

3

35

4–5

5–6

4

5

6

7

8

9

9–10

13

14

15

10

11

12

12–13

15–16

16

17

18

19

20

21

19–20

27–28

25

26

double punch

27

22   double punch   23   24

23–24

28 (first view)   28 (second view)   29

30

31

32 (first view) kiai

34–35

35

36

37

32 (second view) 33 34

32-33 33-34

3-4

Pinan V (Godan)

1 2 3

4   5   6

5-6

9-10

10   11   12

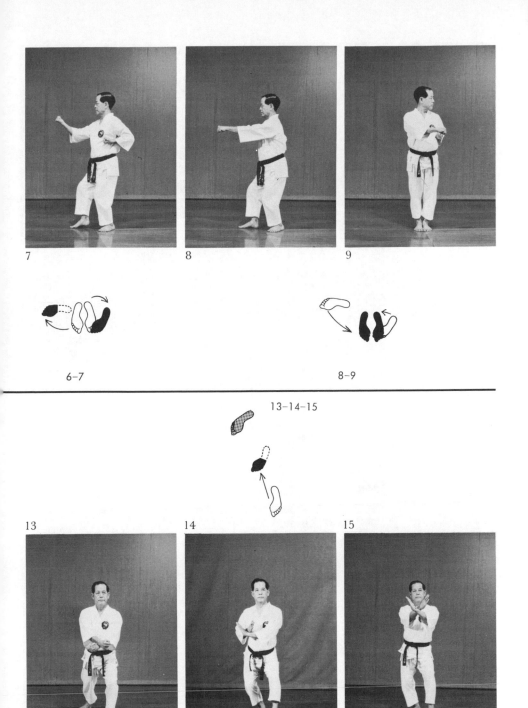

16
17
18 kiai

18-19

21-22

21
22 kiai
23

19 (first view)　　　　19 (second view)　　　　20

20–21

23–24　　　　　　　　　　　　　　　　25–26

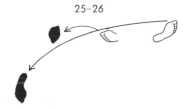

24 (first view)　　　24 (second view)　　　25

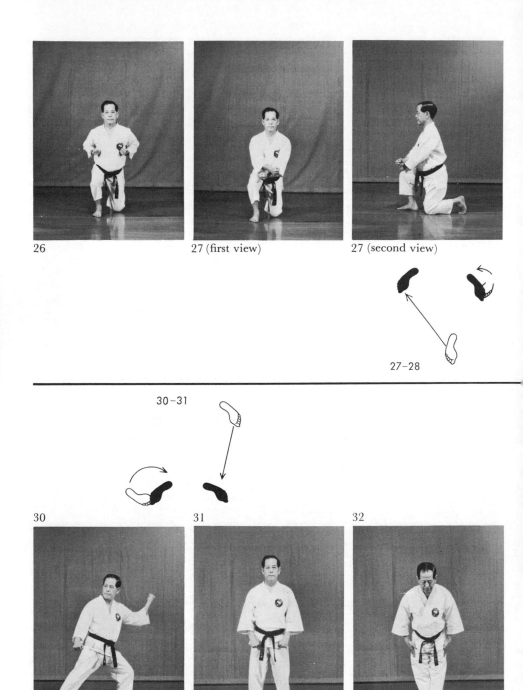

26 27 (first view) 27 (second view)

27–28

30–31

30 31 32

28 (first view) 28 (second view) 29

28–29

29–30

33

1   2

Naihanchi I (Shodan)

内
踏
地

NAIHANCHI I–III (Shodan–Sandan)

As for the kata of Naihanchi (Shodan to Sandan), the composer is still unknown, yet these kata were known to the Shuri and Tomari schools even before the kata of Pinan was invented. This is proved by the fact that beginners used to learn Naihanchi instead of Pinan.

The most important and significant distinction of Naihanchi lies not in developing fighting skills of offense and defense, but in training the lower parts of the body such as the waist and legs through slow and steady sideward movements with maximum strength, and also in building up those muscles indispensable to karate training.

The posture for Naihanchi is much similar to the sitting posture for Zen—pulling back the waist and sitting upright with the shoulders down and chin drawn, with strength concentrated on the abdomen.

This kata is often called *kibadachi* or Tekki, which means "horse riding straddle," in mainland Japan. However, nothing but the term *naihanchi* has been traditional among karatemen in Okinawa.

3   4   5

6   7   8

9   10   11

12   13   14

18   19   20

24   25   26

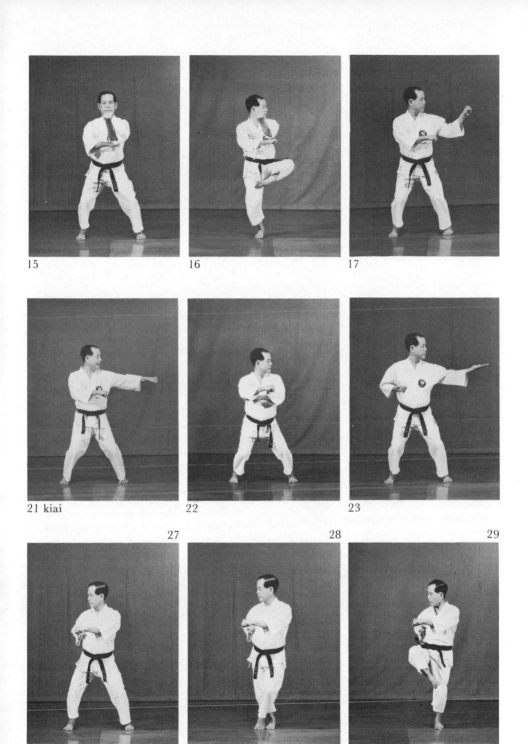

15   16   17

21 kiai   22   23

27   28   29

KATA MOVEMENTS: NAIHANCHI I   **151**

30

31

32

36

37

38 kiai

Naihanchi II (Nidan)

1

2

33   34   35

39   40   41

3   4   5

6   7   8

12   13   14

18   19   20

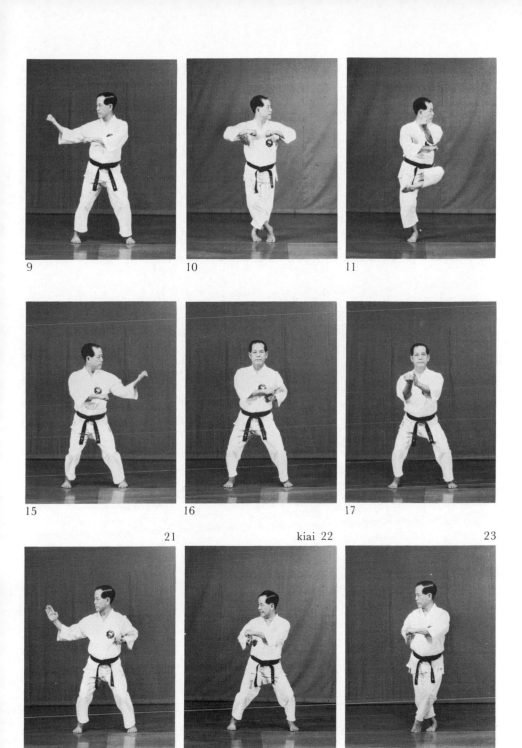

9   10   11

15   16   17

21   kiai 22   23

24

25

26

30

31

32

36

37

38

27

28

29

33

34 kiai

35

39

40

41

42

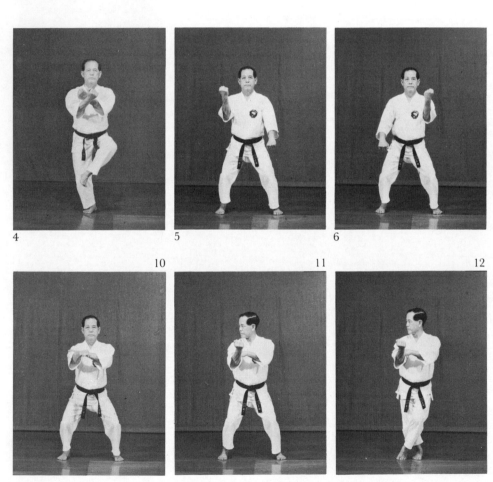

4   5   6

10   11   12

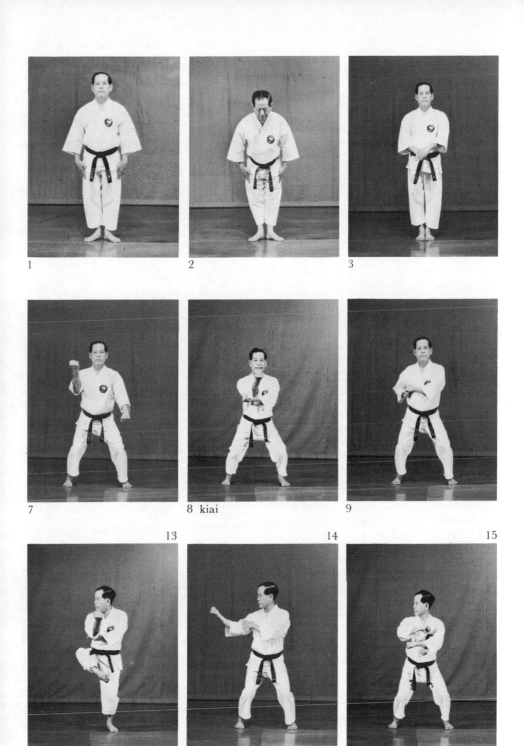

1   2   3

7   8 kiai   9

13   14   15

16 17 18

22 23 24

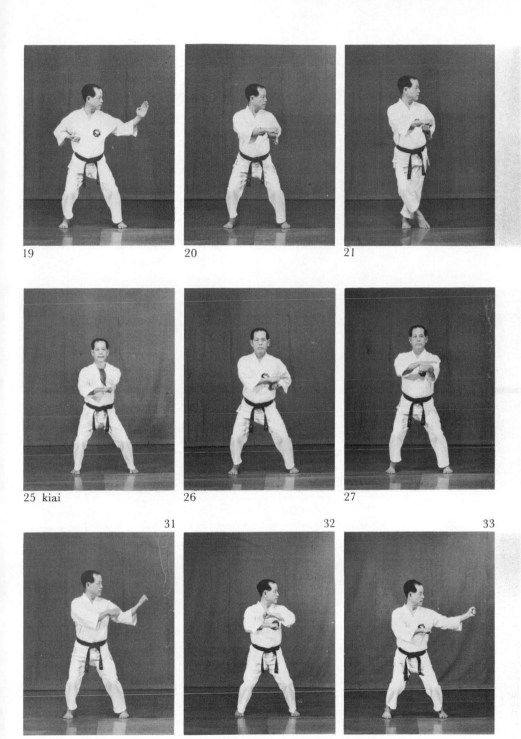

19
20
21

25 kiai
26
27

31
32
33

34   35   36

40   41   42

37

38

39

43

44

45

1
2

安
南
空

ANANKU

The composer of this short kata is unknown, and the history of it is comparatively short. Ananku distinguishes itself from the other kata by offensive and defensive skills with the front-leg-bent stance.

164

3

4

5

3–4–5

6

7

8

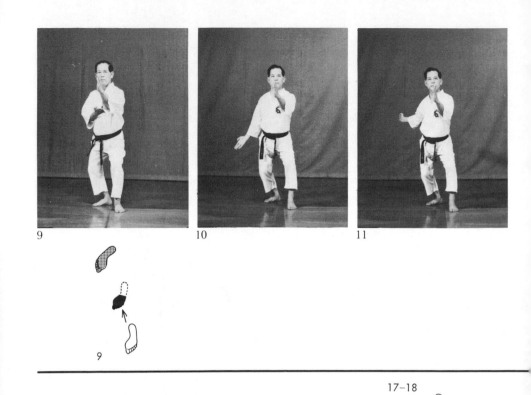

9   10   11

9

17–18

15   16   double punch 17

12

13

14 kiai

19–20

18   19   20

21   22 (first view)   22 (second view)

26–27

26   27 (first view)   27 (second view)

23   24   double punch   25

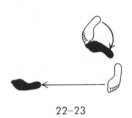

22–23

28   29 kiai   double punch   30

31   32   33

31–32

34

1   2

WANKAN

The composer of this kata is also unknown, however it has a long history. The present kata of Wankan has been inherited by karatemen around Tomari village. The kata is characterized by the unitary sequence of the techniques of offense and defense, which look elegant and powerful.

3   4   5

3–4   4–5

10–11

9   10   11

6   7   double punch   8

5–6   8–9

13–14

12   13   14

15

16

17

22–23

21

22

23

18 kiai   19   20

18–19   19–20

24   25   26

KATA MOVEMENTS: WANKAN   **175**

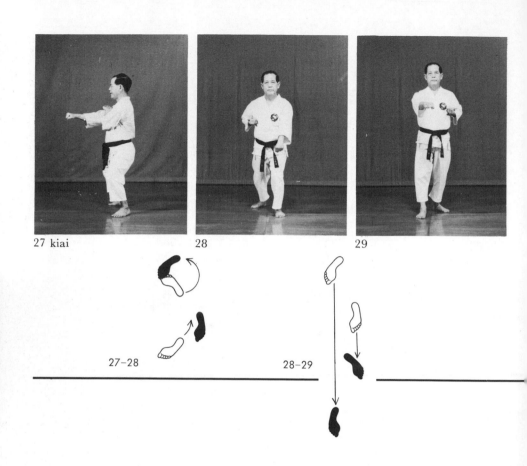

27 kiai   28   29

27–28   28–29

32   33   34

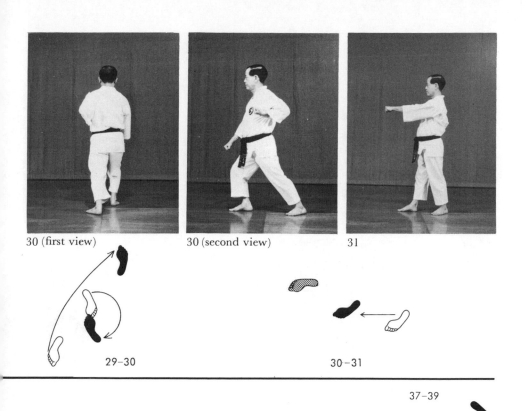

30 (first view)　　　30 (second view)　　　31

29-30　　　　　　　　　　　30-31

37-39

35　　　　　36　　　　　37

38 (first view)

38 (second view)

39

39–40

40

41

42

1   2

ROHAI

Although the composer of this kata is unknown, it has a long history. The present kata of Rohai has been inherited by karatemen around Tomari village. The most characteristic technique of the kata is a one-foot standing stance with the other foot drawn to deliver a kick and to shift the body from an attack.

3   4 (first view)   4 (second view)

4–5

10–11

8   9   10

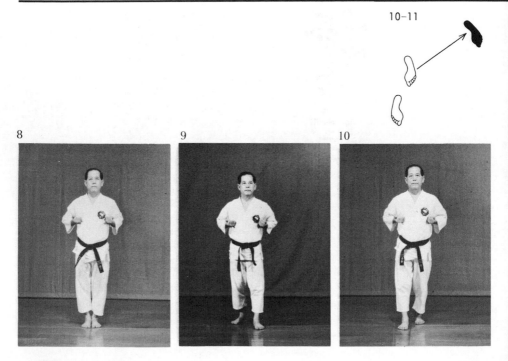

5

6

7

5–6

7–8

11

12

13   double punch →

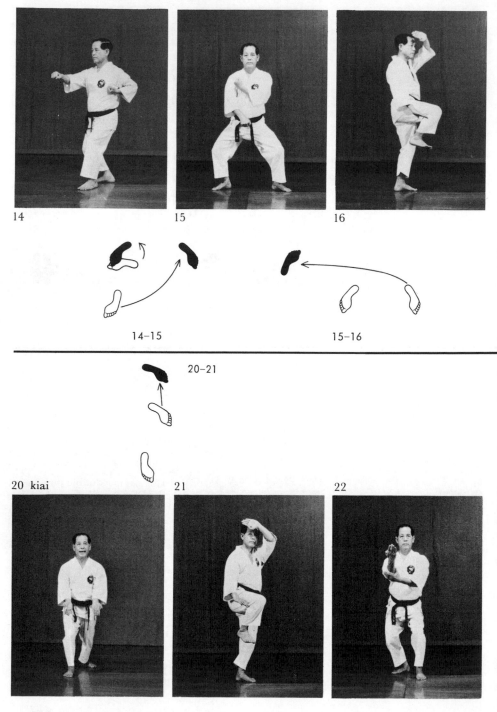

14

15

16

14-15

15-16

20-21

20 kiai

21

22

17   18   double punch   19

19–20

24–25

23   double punch   24   25

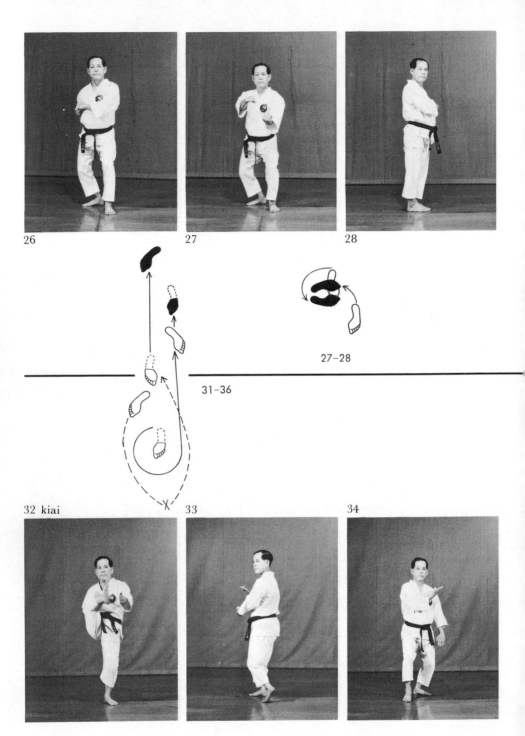

26   27   28

27–28

31–36

32 kiai   33   34

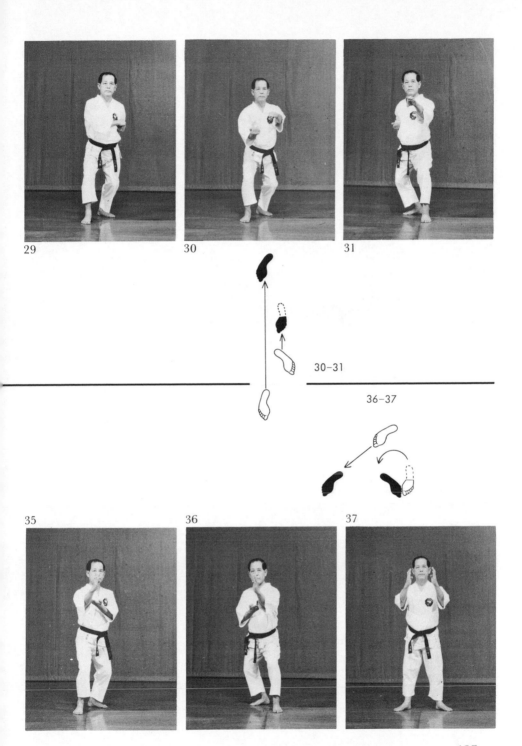

30–31

36–37

38   39   40

38–39

1   2

汪
輯

WANSHU

It is said that this kata was brought into Okinawa in 1683 by a Chinese envoy named Wanshu, and then reformed and developed later by karatemen around Tomari village. The kata was named after the envoy.

Kakushi-zuki (hidden fist punch) is the most significant technique adopted in Wanshu.

3

4

5

5–6

8–9–10

10–11–12

9

10

11

6

7

8

7–8

13

13–14

12

13

14 (first view)

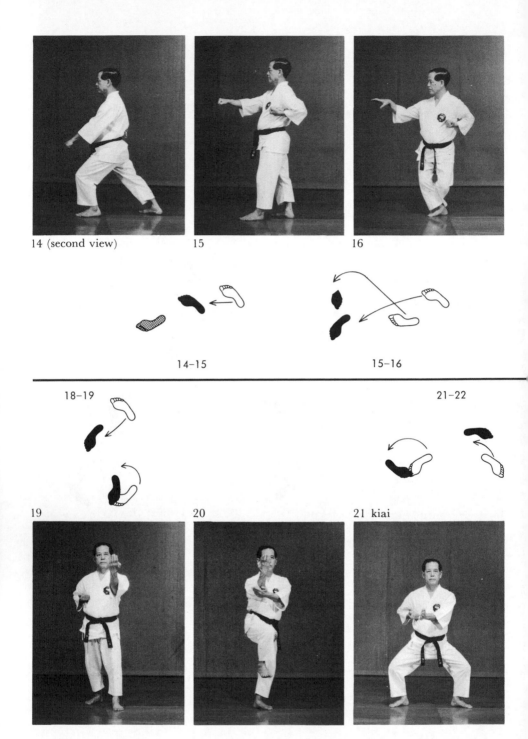

14 (second view)   15   16

14–15   15–16

18–19   21–22

19   20   21 kiai

17

18 (first view)

18 (second view)

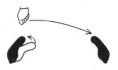

17–18

22

23

24

25

26

27

24–25

26–27

30–31

31–32

31

32 kiai

33

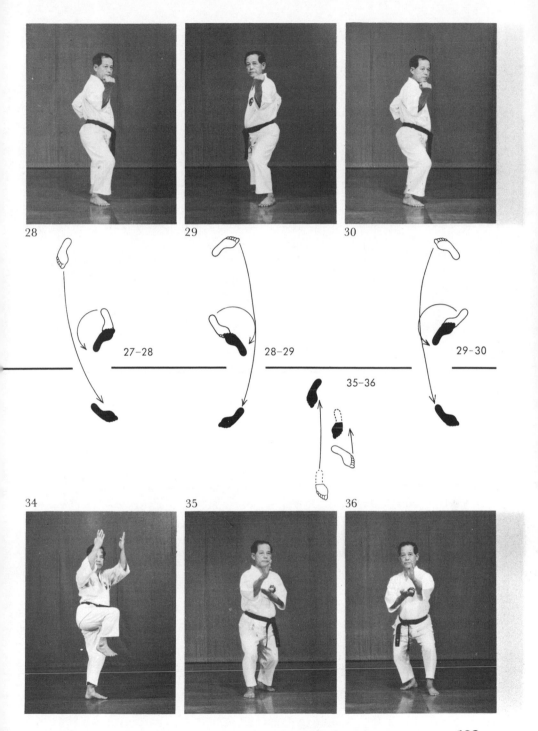

28

29

30

27–28

28–29

29–30

35–36

34

35

36

37 38 39

35–36

1

2

PASSAI

The composer of this dateless kata is unknown. It, however, continues to be cherished by karatemen around Tomari village. *Shuto waza* (knife-hand techniques) and speedy movements distinguish the kata from the others.

This was a favorite of Sensei Kyan.

3

4

5

4–5

8–9

8 (first view)

8 (second view)

9 (first view)

6 (first view)

6 (second view)

7

5–6

10–11

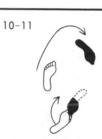

9 (second view)

10

11

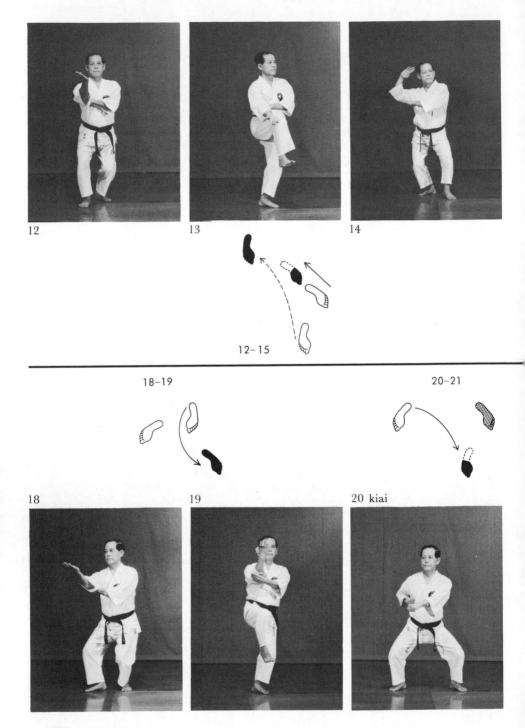

12 13 14

12–15

18–19   20–21

18   19   20 kiai

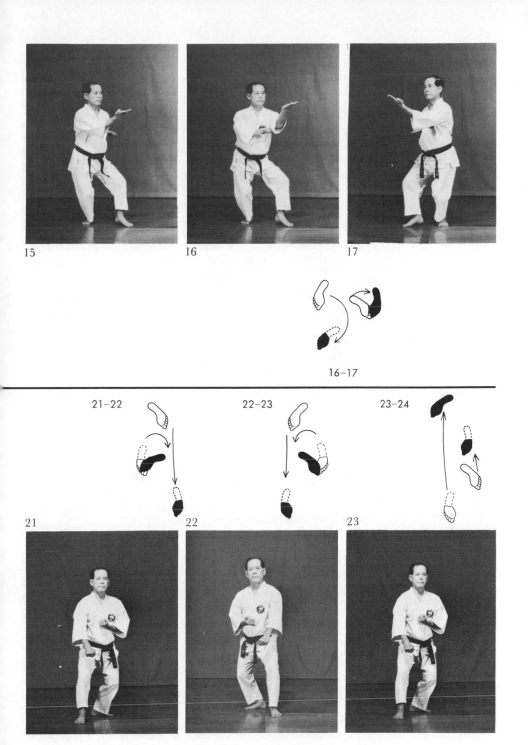

15   16   17

16–17

21–22   22–23   23–24

21   22   23

24

25

26

24-25

29-30

30-31

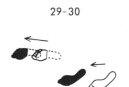

29

30

31

27   28 (first view)   28 (second view)

27–28   28–29

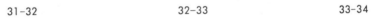

31–32   32–33   33–34

32 kiai   33   34

35

36

37 kiai

34–35

35–36

41–42

42–44

41

42

43

202 CHAPTER V

38

39

40

37–38

44–45

45–47

44

45

46

47

48

49

47–48

52–53

53–54

52

53

54

50 (first view)　　　　50 (second view)　　　51

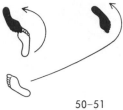

50–51

51–52

54–55

55　　　　　　　56　　　　　　　57

1   2

五
十
四
歩

GOJUSHIHO

This anonymous kata is called Gojushiho, which literally means 54 steps, whose movements are said to resemble those of a drunken man.

Nukite-zuki (spear-hand thrust), one of the open-hand techniques, distinguishes the kata from the others.

206 CHAPTER V

3   4   5

3–4

6–7

6   7   8

9 10 double punch 11

8–9

15 double punch 16 kiai 17

12 kiai   13   14

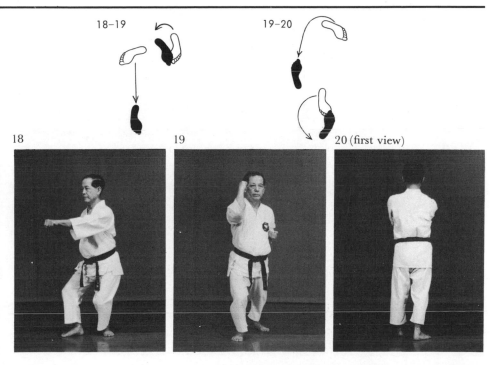

18–19   19–20

18   19   20 (first view)

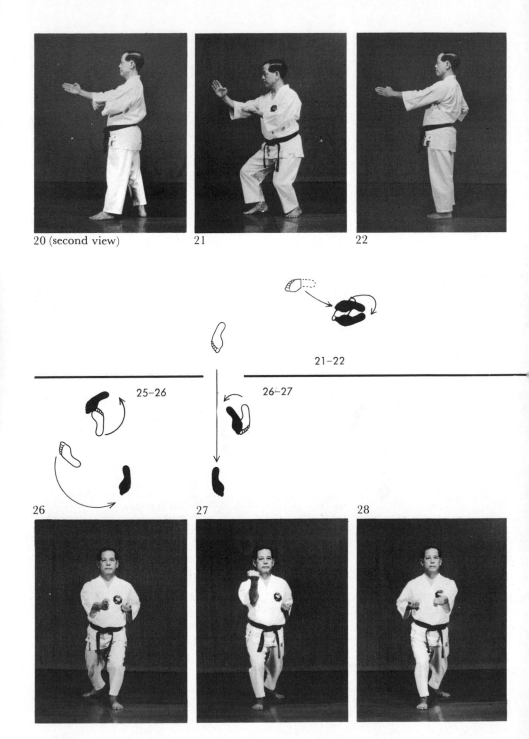

20 (second view)   21   22

21–22

25–26   26–27

26   27   28

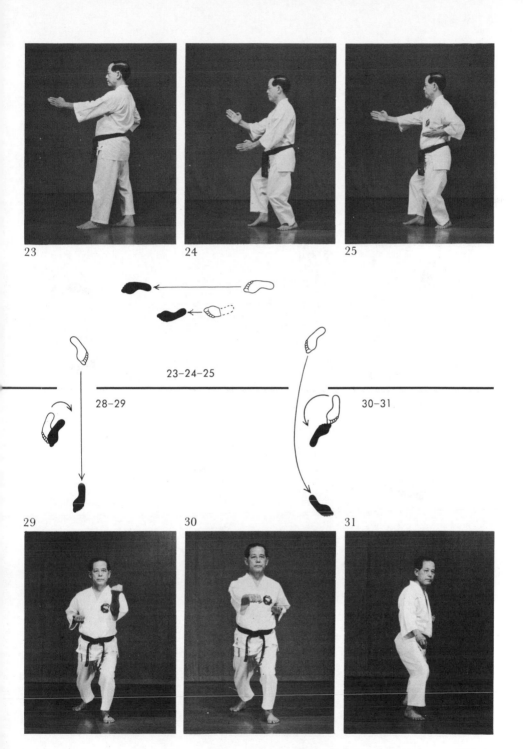

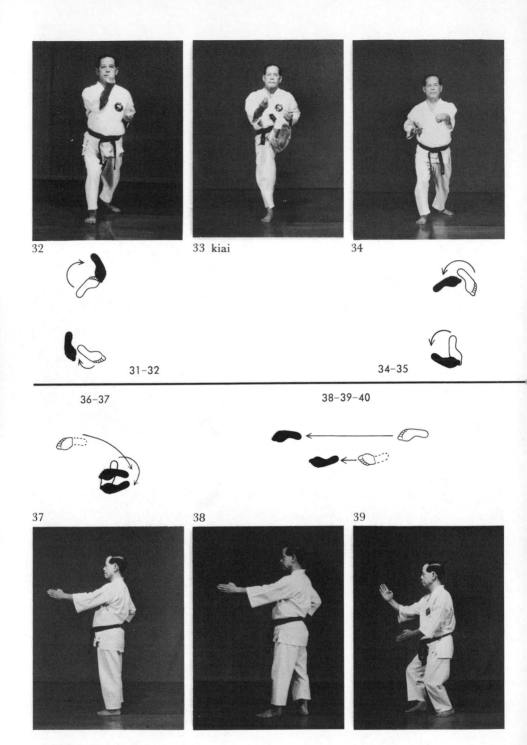

32

33 kiai

34

31–32

34–35

36–37

38–39–40

37

38

39

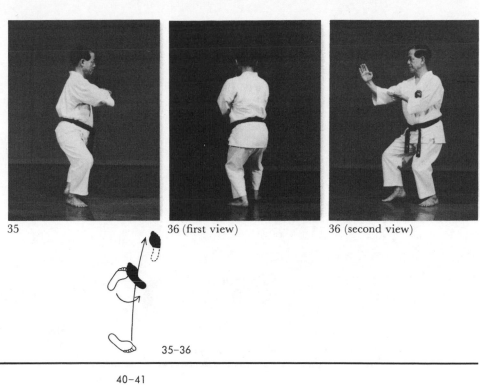

35   36 (first view)   36 (second view)

35–36

40–41

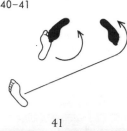

40   41

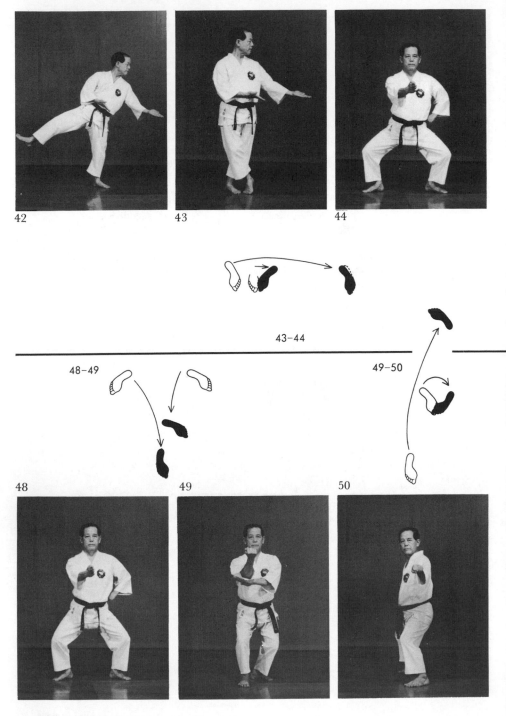

42   43   44

43–44

48–49   49–50

48   49   50

45   46   47

44–45   47–48

50–51   53–54

51   52   53

54   55   56 kiai

54–55   55–56

60

57

58

59

56–57

57–58

1   2

鎮
聞

CHINTO

Chinto, also one of the anonymous kata, is characterized by dynamic movements using kicking techniques including the flying kick and unitary techniques of offense and defense. The kata is simply done through a straight line.

This was also a favorite of Kyan and of Arakaki.

3

4

5

2–3

3–6

6

7

8   double punch →

9   10   11

9-10   10-11

15   16 kiai   17

220 CHAPTER V

12   13   14

11-12

18-19

18   19   20

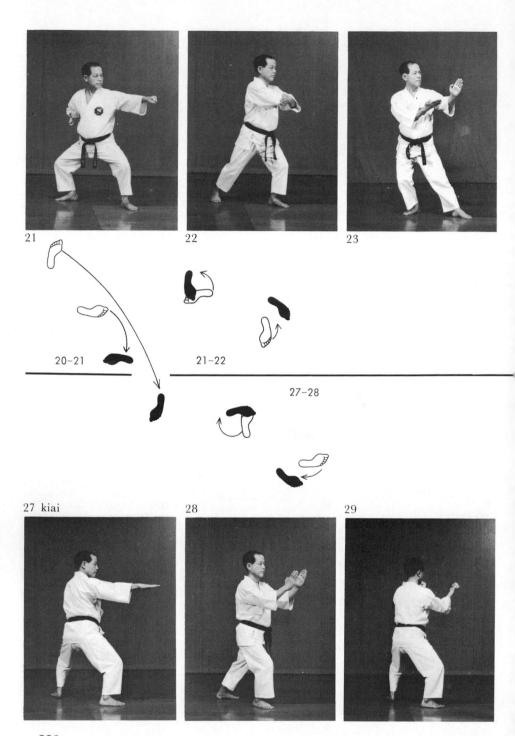

21

22

23

20–21

21–22

27–28

27 kiai

28

29

24   25   26

30-31   32-33

30   31   32

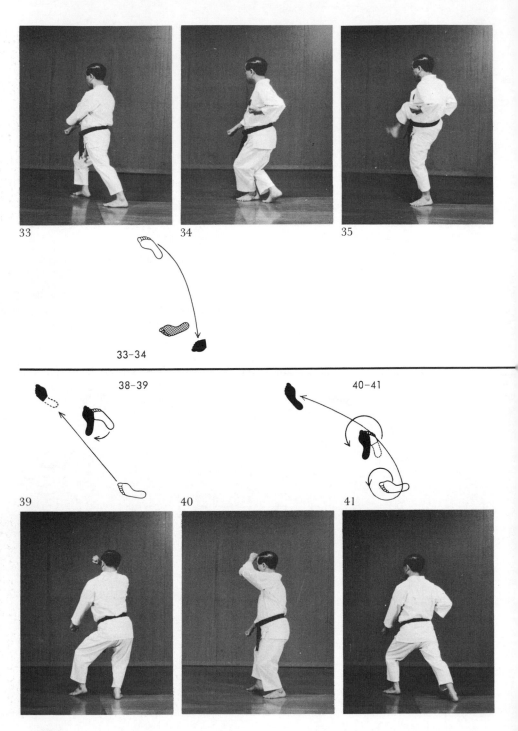

33

34

35

33-34

38-39

40-41

39

40

41

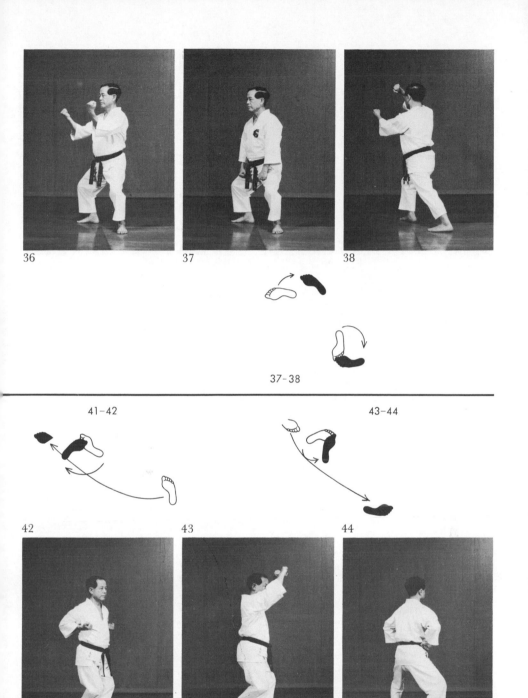

36   37   38

37-38

41-42   43-44

42   43   44

45   46   47

53–54

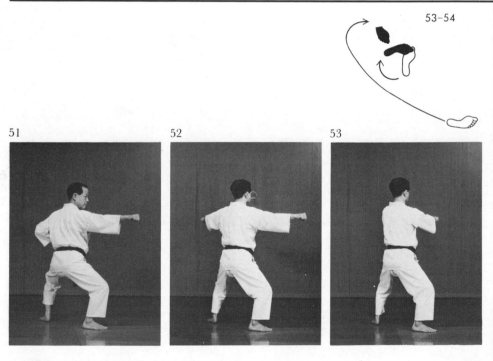

51   52   53

48

49

50 kiai

48–49

54

55

56

57 58 59

57–58

58–59

65–66

63 64 65

60

61 kiai

62

62–63

66

67

1   2

KUSANKU

This kata was adapted and developed by Okinawan karatemen after it was brought into Okinawa in 1761 by a Chinese karateman named Kusanku. Kusanku, often pronounced *kosokun* in mainland Japan, is the most magnificent and advanced kata of all Matsubayashi-ryu karate. Most of the advanced techniques of offense and defense appear in the Kusanku, the longest and most difficult kata, requiring painstaking practice of more than a decade for mastery.

It was the favorite kata of Kyan, who learned it from karateman Yara.

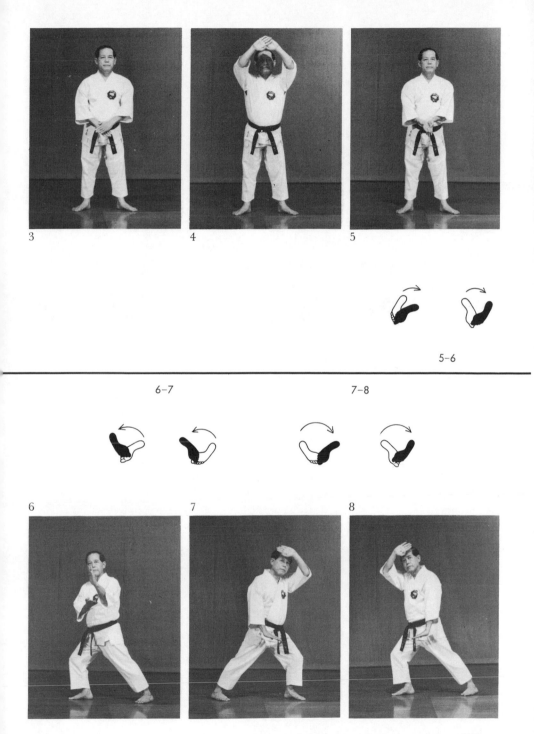

5–6

6–7　　　　　　　7–8

9

10

11

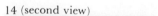

9–10

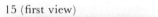

11–12

14 (second view)

15 (first view)

15 (second view)

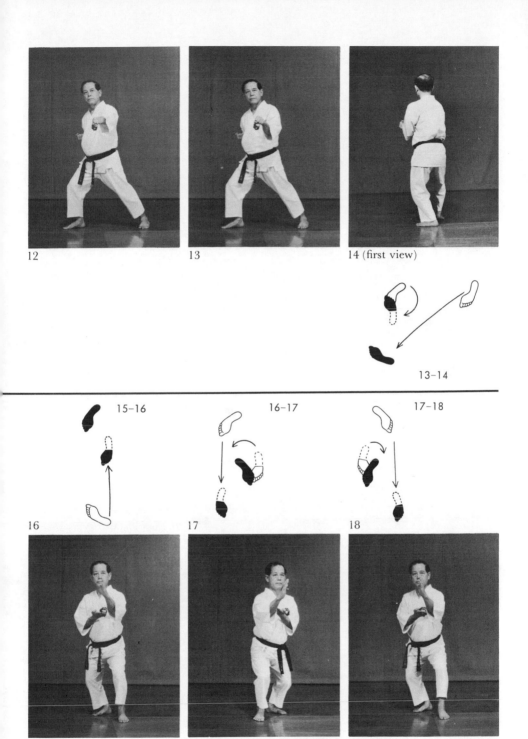

12

13

14 (first view)

13-14

15-16

16-17

17-18

16

17

18

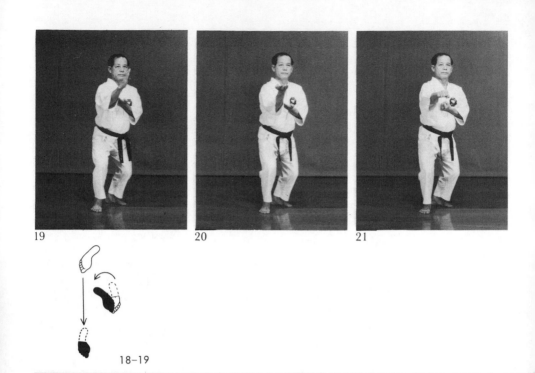

19   20   21

18–19

25–26

24   25   26 (first view)

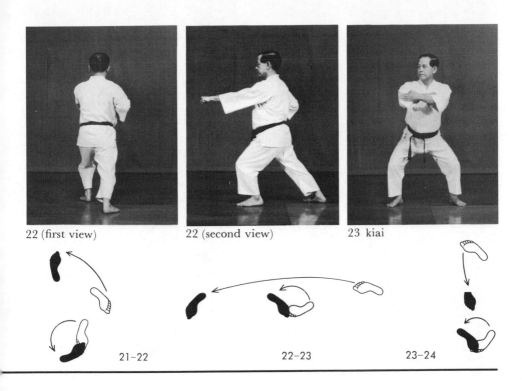

22 (first view)   22 (second view)   23 kiai

21–22   22–23   23–24

26 (second view)   27   28

29   30   31

30-31

36-37

35   36   37

32　　　　　　　　33　　　　　　　　34

33–34

39–40

38　　　　　　　　39　　　　　　　　40

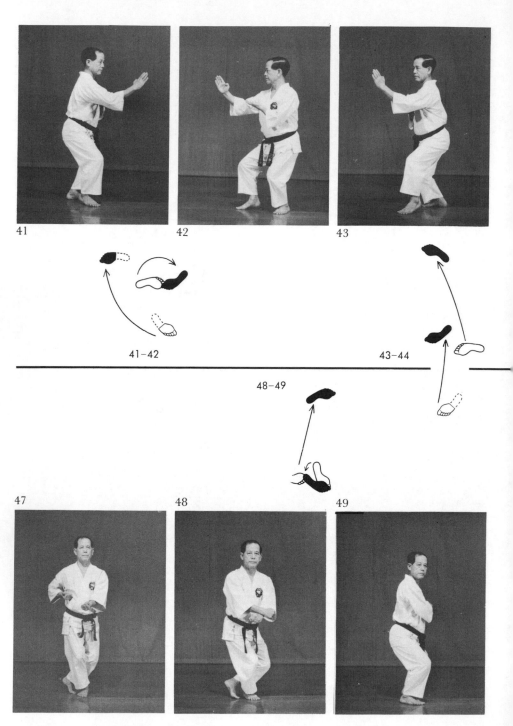

41

42

43

41–42

43–44

48–49

47

48

49

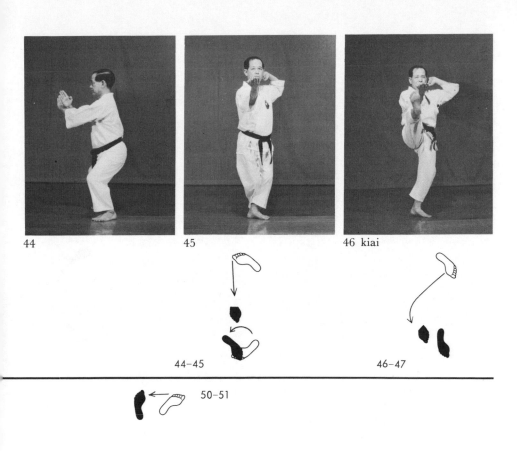

44 45 46 kiai

44-45 46-47

50-51

50 51 (first view) 51 (second view)

52 kiai

53

54

54–55

56–57

57–58

56 (second view)

57

58 kiai

55 (first view)   55 (second view)   56 (first view)

55–56

58–59–61

59   60   61

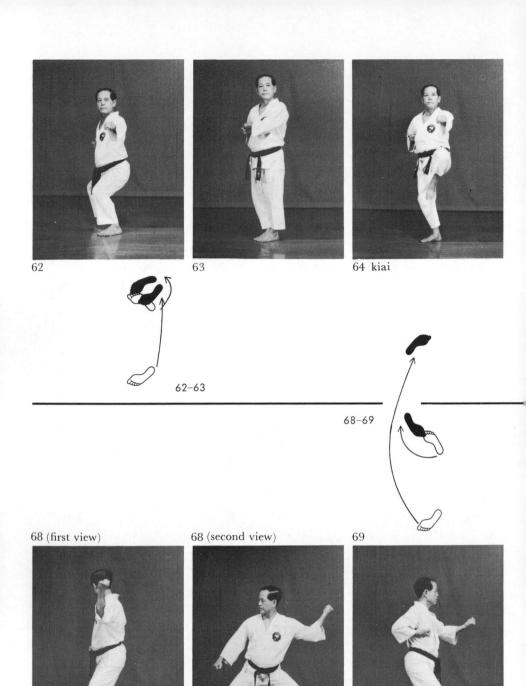

62

63

64 kiai

62–63

68–69

68 (first view)

68 (second view)

69

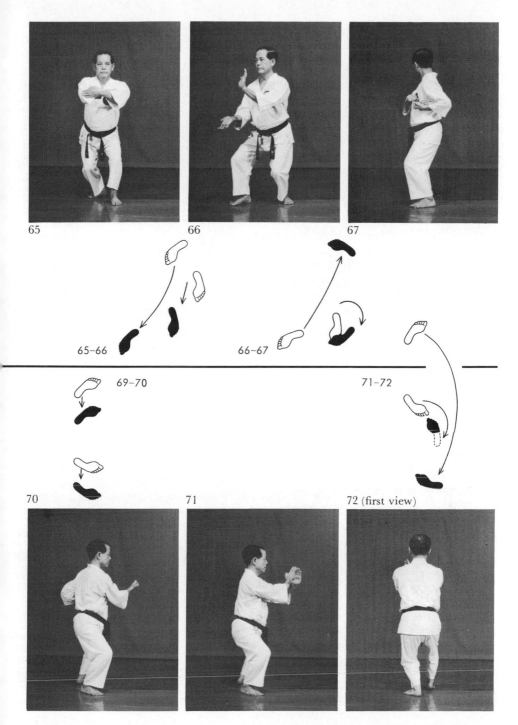

65

66

67

65–66

66–67

69–70

71–72

70

71

72 (first view)

72 (second view) 73 kiai 74

78 79 80

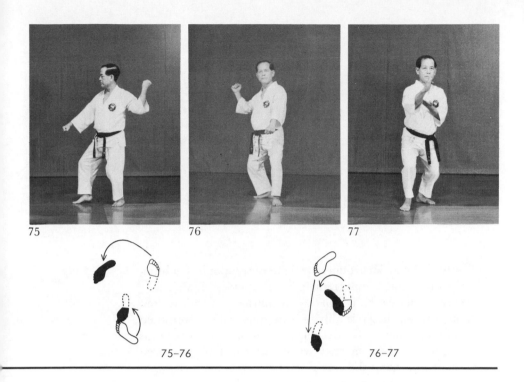

75

76

77

75–76

76–77

VI

On Kumite (Sparring)

Karate is a martial art developed out of weaponless fighting techniques, and it must remain so. This fact demands that we reconsider carefully whether the mastery of kata is itself enough when the possibility of being physically confronted by an opponent or being compelled to defend ourselves is ever present. As a martial art, karate must be practiced without forgetting the existence of the opponent or opponents seeking the opportunity to attack from every angle and in every possible way. The preparation for this attack cannot be achieved through the mastery of kata alone. So practice of *kumite* (sparring) is needed, especially prearranged kumite, which enables one to sharpen his reflexes and fighting sense, to find the proper *ma-ai* and to develop the ability to read an opponent's mind that serves to get the advantage of the opponent in an actual fighting situation.

The most advantageous *ma-ai* is generated by placing the opponent in sight and simultaneously getting out of the opponent's sight. If you simply move back from attacks coming from the front, you give an opening to the opponent's attacks. In other words, the more you move away from the opponent's attacks, the more you will be busy defending yourself from him. Therefore you must be skillful in shifting yourself from side to side so that you can get out of the opponent's sight, placing him in your sight, and making an opening to counterattack. For offensive purposes, body shifting must be done in accordance with the opponent's attack. An attack immediately after the body is shifted is effective and powerful.

246

Modern body-building equipment.

When developing the ability to "read the opponent's mind," you must not set your eyes on any particular part of the opponent, such as his hands, but must always keep his whole figure in your sight so as to "read" his intentions.

Karate must be studied as a martial art with due stress on the practice of kumite as a life-or-death match but not for tournament purposes. As I have always asserted, kata and kumite are to karate as mother and father are to children. Both must be fully studied and practiced with due consideration given to maintaining a properly balanced relationship between them.

The contact with another in kumite practice is invaluable training. The skills one has learned are tested through kumite in the unique mutual relationship established between one's self and the opponent. Testing one's self against another, not with the intention of harming the other or showing off one's skills for tournament purposes, but with the intention of committing one's whole being to the situation, makes kumite a marvelous learning experience. As in kata, self-development is the essence of kumite.

Before kumite practice can be engaged in, however, the student must have developed a sufficient power in atemi. Sufficient power can only be obtained by hard and relentless training of the muscles. The training methods for producing the terrific force of atemi are based on scientific principles. The force of atemi, according to physical dynamics, is directly related to the degree of velocity and mass.

Chishi

Sashi

Kami

Tetsugeta

As velocity and mass are added to a blow of masterful focus and technique, more destructive power is obtained.

Velocity is generally increased by training the extensor and flexor muscles by continuous and repetitive practice of kata, prearranged sparring, and the basic movements. The weight required for the generation of atemi is gained through modern body-building equipment as well as the traditional means of employing *chishi* (an ancient form of dumbbell which looks like a stick with a heavy weight on the end); *sashi* (stone or iron hand grip); *kami* (heavy earthenware jars); and *tetsugeta* (iron clogs).

1   2   3

4   5   6

The force of atemi will be enhanced when both velocity and weight exercises are well balanced. The parts of the body used for atemi—fists, knife-hand, elbows, toes and others—are traditionally hardened or toughened by striking and kicking *makiwara* to such an extent that they become powerful weapons.

The *makiwara* consists of a wooden beam embedded in the ground and rising to about chest height. It is about $4'' \times 2''$ (10 cm. $\times$ 5 cm.) at the bottom and tapers to about $4'' \times 1/2''$ (10 cm. $\times$ 1 cm.) at the top, making it both strong and flexible. The striking portion is often wrapped with a rope made of rice straw. All parts of the body, particularly the fists, are toughened by striking it. The most important function of *makiwara* training is to develop the maximum centrifugal force from the center of the body. When the body rotates with the linear motion of the arm when punching, it achieves maximum momentum behind the punch. A special *makiwara* is used in the photos (Figs. 1–6). The Chinese book *Bubishi* makes no reference to the use of training equipment similar to *makiwara,* so from this it can be reasonably concluded that the development of the striking post is uniquely Okinawan.

It must be understood that unless the parts of the body used for atemi are thoroughly toughened, the force of atemi will not be powerful enough to produce a lethal blow (Figs. 7–11).

When we are ready to practice kumite there are important things to remember. Once confronting the opponent, we must try to forget the difference in *dan* or *kyu** in each other and believe that nobody can be stronger than us as long as we concentrate our senses and minds on finding a way to defeat the opponent, fully utilizing the physical power, intelligence, and karate technique we have so far achieved. This seems to be simple and ordinary, yet it is sometimes neglected and discarded even by the experts. The point I have just made is apt to be forgotten, especially in the practice of *yakusoku kumite* (prearranged sparring). For instance, I have often witnessed kumite in which with one hand one man blocks the opponent's attack and attacks him with the other. Here ends kumite in spite of the fact that further movement of the opponent is possible. Carefully analyzing this type of kumite, we can easily recognize that it could be applied to an actual situation, but it is only, after all, a so-called "artificial or dead kumite" which by prearrangement prohibits the opponent's possible movements after the first attack, so that one man can assume that he blocks and attacks, and finally beats the opponent.

The fact is that we should not assume any discontinuation of the opponent's movement since he would, in an actual situation, likely continue his movements, and perhaps even emerge as the victor. Our attitude in practicing prearranged kumite should, therefore, be based strongly on the premise that our opponent is likely to try to block our counterattack

* *Kyu* and *dan* refer to karate ranks. *Kyu* ranks are all those below the black belt rank and *dan* ranks are all ranks of first degree black belt and above.

7

8

9 10 11

and continue to fight. We should also, as part of our mental attitude in practicing kumite, bear strongly in mind that our opponent may vary his attack, and endeavor to be always prepared to defend against such variations.

Motobu, my sensei, used to preach against "dead kumite." Therefore, I deliberately developed kumite, seriously considering the following seven essential conditions:

1. To develop techniques to enable us to defend and attack simultaneously.

2. To develop techniques to enable us to defend and attack simultaneously using both hands.

3. To develop techniques to enable us to defend and attack simultaneously using both hands and feet.

4. To develop techniques to enable us to shift the body to the attacking position reflexively and naturally in order to always keep beside the opponent and avoid facing him.

5. To develop techniques to enable us to defend and attack by means of shifting the body and approaching the opponent from the side or front, with definite determination to find some way of beating the opponent, in critical situations.

6. To develop swift, reflexive nerves or senses which enable us to kick the opponent when he catches us or when we catch him.

7. To develop techniques to enable us to attack the opponent by kick or blow, reflexively, after we have suppressed his movement without losing our grasp on him.

Kumite of Matsubayashi-ryu is the application of the above seven conditions.

As stated previously, prearranged kumite must be practiced as a life-or-death match, but never with the intention of harming the fellow practitioner. In kumite you must commit yourself totally, and from this commitment arises the realization that your blow could easily kill your opponent, that the karateman holds life and death in his hands. But you must never engage in pre-arranged kumite with the intent to kill. The realization that you hold life and death in your hands should lead you to the reaffirmation of life— your own and your opponent's.

Kumite is a unique act of sharing, for with your opponent you are reaching out together toward the total commitment of self and toward the understanding of that commitment. Both of you are striving to exert to the maximum human capacity and to test each other to the fullest. When two people practicing kumite are striving together toward total commitment, a mutual relationship is established in which perfect communication becomes possible even though not a word is spoken. From this striving can come the realization that you have committed yourself and the understanding of that commitment. Most of all, it is an experience of human warmth in which karate grows to be karate-do.

At this point it might be well to mention the differences between karate and karate-do. Karate refers to a martial art developed for the purpose of defending one's self from imminent and illegal violence with the use of the strictly-trained body as a weapon. Karate-do, however, means a way of life based on karate or karate-life, in which one conquers himself and comes off a winner without any use of the art in a strict sense. In other words, its significance lies in fighting down the inner enemies, which are greater than the external enemies, by building up a sound body and mind through painstaking discipline of body and mind by means of karate practice. In short, it can be said that karate-do aims at building up the "whole man" by karate training lasting the remainder of one's life. These considerations are summarized in the words: there is no first attack in karate.

On the following pages the sequential movements of pre-arranged kumite are described.

i

ii

iii

YAKUSOKU KUMITE I–VII

Each kumite set begins and ends with a bow (Figs. i–vi), but this will be shown in Kumite I and VII only. In all the photographs, Jokei Kushi is the attacker and the author is defending. All of the kumite can be executed beginning with either hand and either foot.

254 CHAPTER VI

Yakusoku Kumite I

The attacker punches first to the face (Fig. 2); the defender steps back, using *jodan uke* (Fig. 2), then counterattacks by stepping-in and punching *(oi-zuki)* to the chest (Fig. 3). The attacker now steps back, using *gedan-barai uke* (down block) (Fig. 3), and punches a final punch to the face (Fig. 4). Now the defender, using good timing, punches inside the oncoming fist, toward the opponent's face (Fig. 4). His arm effectively blocks the oncoming fist by this well-timed punch.

1   2   3   4   5

Yakusoku Kumite II

The attacker punches three times to the chest, stepping in each time with *zenkutsu* stance (Figs. 2–5). The defender blocks the first two punches with a down block, while stepping back in natural stance, sliding if necessary. For the third attack, he blocks the punch and strikes at the neck at the same time.

Yakusoku Kumite III

The attacker uses a wide open-leg stance, first punching to chest (Fig. 2). Without stepping again, he punches to the face (Figs. 3, 4). The defender blocks first with inside chest block (Fig. 2). He then blocks the face punch and at the same time, holds back the opponent's fist, which is in its usual ready position (Fig. 3). Now the defender is free to strike with the elbow smash to the ribs.

1

2

3

Yakusoku Kumite IV

The defender takes three natural steps as if walking in the street (Figs. 1–3). Here, he begins with the right foot. The attacker follows, and on the third step, grabs the left shoulder with the right hand (Fig. 4). The defender grasps the opponent's hand (Figs. 5–7) turning around. The attacker punches *jodan-zuki* (upper punch) (Fig. 7), then *chudan-zuki* (middle punch), without stepping. The defender blocks both punches with the same hand, and punches the attacker's chest with the right fist (Fig. 8).

4

5

6

7

8

1

2

Yakusoku Kumite V

The attacker steps in reverse punch *zenkutsu* stance
(Fig. 2). The defender blocks this first punch using reverse
hand *zenkutsu* stance (Fig. 2). The attacker kicks (Fig. 3) and
when his kick is blocked with the same hand that blocked
the punch, turns around into *zenkutsu* stance again (Fig. 4).
The opponents are now facing each other in a ready position (Fig. 5). The attacker steps in *zenkutsu* stance, punching
for the last time. The defender blocks and kicks at the same
time. He uses an open-hand side block that effectively blocks
the punch, and at the same time grabs the opponent's arm,
pulling him into the kick (Figs. 6, 7).

3

4

5

6

7

1

2

Yakusoku Kumite VI

The attacker assumes a fighting stance, then the defender takes a ready position (Fig. 2). They shadow each other's movements, watching carefully, moving first to the left two steps, then to the right, then back (Figs. 3, 4). Now the attacker steps in and punches (Fig. 5). But the defender steps back, slapping the punch down first with the right hand (Fig. 6), then the left hand (Fig. 7), preparing for a backfist strike to the face. This right-left-backfist technique is a common combination that must be speedily executed (Fig. 8).

3

4

5

6

7

8

Yakusoku Kumite VII

The attacker grabs the defender by the collar (Fig. 2). The defender blocks openhanded, as shown, not trying to knock the attacker's arm away, but leading him into the next move. The attacker pushes the defender two steps forward and two steps backward (Figs. 2–4) before punching to the chest (Fig. 5). Now the open hand moves down to block the punch, while the fist punches to the face (Fig. 7).

5

6

7

iv

v

vi

VII

Kobujutsu
(Ancient Weapon Art)

A general treatment of the subject of Matsubayashi-ryu karate-do would not be complete without touching on the subject of *kobujutsu* (ancient weapon art).

As I hope to publish another volume in the future concerning kobujutsu along with a discussion of the relationship between Zen and karate-do, I will include here only a few basic comments on the art.

Kobujutsu developed as an art of self-defense during periods in Okinawan history when the country was under subjugation and weapons were not permitted. With typical ingenuity, the Okinawans learned to fight without weapons, or with whatever came to hand during times of conflict. With the possible exception of the *sai,* a metal sword-blocking instrument, what did come to hand were articles found in day-to-day use in feudal times: the *bo, nunchaku, tuifa,* and *kama.* The *kama,* a hand sickle, is still widely used as a farming implement in Okinawa today.

These weapons have been incorporated in Okinawan karate and the art associated with their use is now practiced as supplementary kata training by students who have mastered the basic forms sufficiently to find such supplementary training valuable.

Bo-jutsu

The *bo* is a staff of hard wood about six feet (180 cm.) long, about one inch (2.5 cm.) in diameter, and slightly tapered at the ends. It was originally used as a tool to carry

Fighting postures using the bo.

loads and also served as a fighting tool when the occasion demanded.

The use of the *bo* in martial arts has developed two variations; one is preserved in a kind of folk dance presented at local festivals while the other is practiced as a genuine martial art.

In Okinawa there exist more than ten varieties of the art of *bo*, most of which have been considerably popularized.

KOBUJUTSU **267**

Defensive postures with nunchaku.

Nunchaku

The *nunchaku* is a pair of hard wooden sticks with a cord attached at the end. The centrifugal force produced by swinging the *nunchaku* makes it an effective weapon.

Though less powerful than the *bo,* the *nunchaku* is more convenient to carry because of its smaller size, but it is not always a handy weapon because of difficulty in manipulating it. Skillful use calls for a considerable amount of practice, and insufficient practice may result in self-inflicted injury. A veteran, of course, can skillfully manipulate *nunchaku* blindfolded, as if the sticks were part of his body.

Fighting postures using the tuifa.

Tuifa

Tuifa refers to two pieces of rectangular hard wood, each about 16 inches (40 cm.) long, with a grip attached. By grasping the grips, one can manipulate them for defensive and offensive purposes by swinging, striking, or thrusting.

Defensive postures with the sai.

Sai-jutsu

The iron weapon *sai*, which in older days officials used to arrest criminals and to hold back crowds, was actually invented to defend against attacks from swords, *bo, nunchaku,* or *tuifa*. A pair of iron sticks about 16 inches long with U-shaped handles, the *sai* are the heaviest of this group of weapons. A veteran could manipulate them quite easily, however, as if he were using wooden sticks.

Afterword

Karate-do has become international in scope. From the small island of Okinawa it has spread to all parts of the world. The way of karate can be followed by anyone—man, woman, or child—and through karate training one can attain the highest ideals of beauty and strength. This beauty and strength is both inner and outer, mental and physical.

Amidst the noise and rapid changes of modern society, one can find in karate-do a peace of mind that will never be shaken. Through karate training one acquires stoicism and self-control which will prepare him fully to meet life's many responsibilities. Karate training takes devotees along the path of self-development. Every movement, every step in karate training requires one to make a total commitment of self. Complete and unswerving focus and power in karate practice help one to understand himself because he is required to fuse his entire being through physical motion. Because the self, in all its aspects and complexities, must be totally committed in karate training, the ability to commit the self will also carry over into all aspects of life. Karate training helps to end a dualistic way of life in which a person is separated by lack of commitment from the world around him. From this comes peace of mind.

The fusing of mind and body in karate is indescribably beautiful and spiritual. The flow of the mind, when totally absorbed during kata practice, brings a person into total contact with the essence and core of his being. One is both humbled and uplifted by this knowledge of self.

All of the spiritual aspects of karate-do and the ways in which it can bring one to self-realization cannot be fully described. I have pursued the study of karate in an attempt to bring karate and Zen together as one. This has been a life-long effort, and one that can never be fully realized by any one person. My pursuit of karate has brought me a limited understanding of the way to self-realization, however, and I hope to be able to share my experience with others throughout the world.

In the near future, I hope to write another book concerning the critical connection between karate and Zen as expressed in *ken zen ichijo,* "Karate and Zen as one."

Glossary-Index

elbow block: see *hiji-uke*

finger technique: see *yubi waza*
fist technique: see *seiken waza*
forearm block: see *seiken-ude-uke*
fukubu-geri (abdomen kick)   96
fukyūgata (a Matsubayashi-ryū kata) 59, 103, 104; pictorial sequences of   104–15
Funakoshi, Gichin   21, 22, 24, 34

gedan-barai-uke   (down block)   255
gedan haitō-yoko-uke (lower sideward reverse knife-hand block)   93
gedan kōsa-uke (lower cross block)   86
gedan shōtei-ate (lower palm-heel smash)   80
gedan shōtei-uke (lower palm-heel block)   94
gedan shutō-uke (lower knife-hand block)   90
gedan shutō-yoko-barai-uke (lower sideward knife-hand slashing block)   90
gedan-uke (lower block)   84
gedan yoko-barai-uke (lower sideward block)   84
gedan-zuki (lower punch)   70
Gojū-ryū (one of original Okinawan karate schools)   22
gojūshiho (a Matsubayashi-ryū kata) 58, 103, 206; pictorial sequence of   206–17
Gusukuma, Shinpan   24, 35

haitō-uchi (reverse knife-hand strike)   78
haitō-uke (reverse knife-hand block)   89–93
Hanashiro, Chōmo   24, 35
hangetsu-barai-uke   (half-moon foot block)   95

hazushi-uke (removing block)   88
heian: see *pinan*
heisoku-dachi (closed-foot stance)   60, 63
hidari-ashi-mae   shizentai-dachi (left-foot-front natural stance)   62
Higaonna, Kanryō   20
hiji (elbow)   27
hiji-ate (elbow smash)   78
hiji-uke (elbow block)   95
hiza-ate (knee smash)   80
hotoke-gamae   (Buddha-hand fighting posture)   101

iaigoshi-dachi (kneeling stance)   68
intermediate movements: history of   99; postures of 100–103;   purpose of 99–100, 102
ippon-ashi-dachi (one-leg stance)   68
Itosu, Ankō   24, 40, 116

jigotai-dachi   (wide   open-leg stance)   61, 65, 66
jōdan kōsa-uke (upper cross block)   86
jōdan shōtei-ate (upper palm-heel smash)   80
jōdan uchi-shutō-uke (upper inner knife-hand block)   90
jōdan-uke (upper block) 82, 255
jōdan wari-uke (upper split block)   84
jōdan-zuki (upper punch)   41, 70, 258
jōsokutei (ball of the foot)   96
jun shizentai-dachi (quasi-natural stance)   63

kakushi-zuki (hidden fist punch)   71, 187
kaku-zuki (square punch)   70

kama (hand sickle)   266

kamaekata (ready stances)   57–60

kāmi (heavy earthenware jars)   248

kansetsu-geri (kicks aimed at joints)   26

karate (empty-handed self-defense art)   24; attitudes for training in 48–49; ethics of 49; history of 19–21, 24–26; masters of 20, 21, 24, 31–46, 104, 116, 218, 230; popularization of 24–26; precepts and maxims of 47, 48, 64, 82; study recommendations for 29–30; styles of 21–24; tournament system of 27–29; training hints in 49–51

karate-dō (way of karate)   19, 47, 69

karate-gi (karate uniform)   49

kata (form in karate practice) 19, 55–56; basic movements of 56–98; intermediate movements of 99–102; pictorial sequences of 194–245; sequential movements of 103

keikoken-zuki (forefinger-knuckle punch)   45

kentsui (hammer fist)   75

kentsui-uchi (hammer-fist strike) 76

keri waza (kicking technique) 26

kerikata (kicking techniques): examples of 96–98; strategy of 96

kiai (life force, inner strength) 27

kibadachi (horse-riding straddle): see *naihanchi*

kicking techniques: see *kerikata*

kime waza (winning techniques) 27

kinteki-geri (groin kick)   96

knife-hand block: see *shutō-uke*

kobujutsu (ancient weapon art) 35, 266; examples of 266–70

kōkutsu-dachi (back-leg-bent stance)   67

kōsa-dachi (cross-leg stance)   67

koshi o ireru ("putting in the hip," twisting hip movement)   61

Kuba, Chōjin   31

kumite (sparring): conditions for developing 252; development of 42; preparation for 19, 246–50, 252–53; sequential movements in 254–64

kumite match   26–27

Kūsankū   21, 230

kūsankū (a Matsubayashi-ryū kata) 21, 58, 103, 230; pictorial sequence of 230–45

Kyan, Chōtoku 24, 32, 35, 36, 39–42, 218, 230

kyōbu-geri (chest kick)   96

kyōbu morote shutō-uchi (chest double knife-hand strike) 77

kyōbu shutō-uchi (chest knife-hand strike)   77

kyōbu-soete shutō-uchi (chest augmented knife-hand strike) 77

kyū (karate rank below black belt)   250

ma-ai (ready distance between opponents)   246

Mabuni, Kenwa   24

magetori-barai-uke (rising upward both-hand knife block) 92

makite-uke (winding knife-hand block)   92

makiwara (striking or punching board)   70, 249–50

sasae-uke (supported forearm block) 84

sāshī (stone or iron hand-grip) 29, 248

sayū-barai-uke (double lower side block) 84

sayū-zuki (double side punch) 71

seiken (fist) 20, 69, 70–71, 75

seiken-ude-uke (forearm block) 82–88

seiken waza (fist technique) 69

seiza (formal sitting position) 68

semekata (attacking techniques) 69–81: with elbow 78; with fist 69–73, 75–76, 82; with hand 74, 75–78, 80; with knee 80

sensei (teacher, instructor) 35, 36

shigoki (savage training) 28

Shimabuku, Tarō 31, 36

shizentai-dachi (natural stance) 61–62

shi-zuki (beak thrust) 74

Shōrei-ryū (ancient karate style) 21–22; *see also* Naha-te

Shōrin-ryū (one of original Okinawan karate schools) 21–23; *see also* Shuri-te

shōtei (heel of the palm) 80

shōtei-ate (palm-heel smash) 80

shōtei-uke (palm-heel block) 94

Shuri-te (original karate developed in Shuri area) 21–24, 103; *see also* Shōrin-ryū

shutō-uchi (knife-hand strike) 76

shutō-uke (knife-hand block) ·89–93

shutō waza (knife-hand techniques) 195

smashing technique: see *ate waza*

sokkō (instep of the foot) 96

sokutō (foot edge) 98

sokutō-geri (foot-edge kick) 98

soto-hachiji shizentai-dachi (open-leg natural stance) 57, 62

stances: see *tachikata*

striking technique: see *uchi waza*

suirakan no kamae (drunkard fighting-posture) 101

tachikata (stances) 61; examples of 61–68

tate hiji-ate (upward elbow smash) 78

te (hands; precursor of modern Okinawan karate) 19–21

Teijunsoku, poem by 20

tekki: see *naihanchi*

tenshin (body shifting) 101

tenshin no kamae (body-shifting fighting posture) 101

tetsugeta (iron clogs) 248

Tokuda, Anbun 24

Tomari-te (karate developed in Tomari area) 103

tomoe shōtei-ate (circular palm-heel smash) 80

tomoe-zuki (circular block and punch) 70

torite-uke (grasping-hand block) 93

Tō-te (Chinese self-defense art) 20–21, 24

tsuki waza (punching technique): see *seiken waza* 69–71

tsumasaki-geri (toe-tip kick) 38, 96

tuifa (a pair of wooden boards used as a weapon) 266, 269

uchi waza (striking technique) 75: with fist 75, 76; with knife-hand 76–78

Uechi-ryū (a school of modern Okinawan karate) 22